Dear fear,

18 Powerful Lessons On Living Your Best Life
On The Other Side Of Fear

Tiana Patrice
Visionary Author

Tiana Patrice
info@tianapatrice.com

Ordering Information:
Quantity sales: Special discounts are available on quantity purchases by corporations, associations, and nonprofits. For details, contact the publisher at the address above.

Published by KLC Publishing
Designed By: P2P Branded – www.p2pbranded.com

Professional Photography and Videography Provided By:
Phase One Photography
Aprill Jones Photography

Makeup By: Beat By Tip

This book is intended to push you from the place that fear is attempting to keep you bound. This book is not intended to provide financial, health or legal advice. Please seek the appropriate counsel for financial, health or legal matters.

"For God hath not given us the spirit of fear; but of power, and of love, and of a sound mind"

~2 Timothy 1:7~
KJV

Table Of Contents

How To Use This Book:

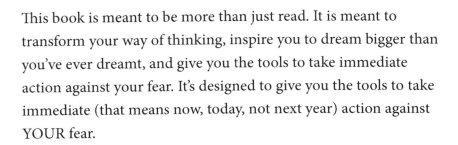

This book is meant to be more than just read. It is meant to transform your way of thinking, inspire you to dream bigger than you've ever dreamt, and give you the tools to take immediate action against your fear. It's designed to give you the tools to take immediate (that means now, today, not next year) action against YOUR fear.

Aren't you ready to take action? Aren't you ready to stop allowing fear to keep you playing small and breathing in the air of mediocrity? You are bold. You are royal. You are deserving. You are excellent. And fear, has no more power over your life.

Step 1: Take some time and write your own letter to fear: Acknowledging the fear allows you to create a strategic plan of action against it.

Dear Fear,

_____

_____

_____

_____

_____

_____

_____

_____

_____

_____

_____

_____

_____

_____

_____

Signed,

_____

Step 2: Take a quick photo of your letter against fear, and head over to social media. Post your photo and tag using #DearFearBook #ActivateYourFearless #AMillionFearlessStrong

Step 3: Join the movement over at www.amillionfearlesstrong.org and invite 5 of your friends to join with you. Together we are A Million Fearless Strong.

We are on a mission to liberate women from the fear that's holding them back in life, career and business.

So join the movement!

A Message from the Visionary Author

Hello Fearless Leader,

I'm so grateful that you are deciding to embark on an exciting journey of activating your fearLESS and beginning to live your best life on the other side of fear. This journey is an exciting one. It's not always an easy one. But it's necessary. Your "New Thing" that God has for you is on the other side of your fear. Your Victory is on the other side of your fear. Your Winning Season is on the other side of your fear. You can't tell me that's not something to be excited about!! I'm amped up for you!

Why? Because I know what it feels like to be plagued by feelings of defeat, overwhelm and self-sabotaging thoughts. I know what it feels like to want to take the "leap" but you don't because you are unsure what's on the other side. I know what it feels like to be your own worst critic. I get it. I know that fear is a consistent hustler and will hustle you out of your hopes and dreams, like the enemy coming in to kill, steal and destroy. But here is what I also know…I know that God has given you the provisions for the vision. I know that God didn't bring you this far to just leave you stranded without the tools, people, and resources to get you to your "New Thing". I know that on the other side of what fear is trying to keep you from is abundance, freedom, joy, and possibilities. And it all belongs to you. Don't allow fear to keep you from your inheritance.

In this book Dear Fear Volume 2, we have pulled together 17 brilliant women who are telling you their stories of how fear attempted to keep them shackled, but how God pulled them out. They are sharing their tools with you, and strategies to reach back and pull you forward. If you ask them, they will tell you that this journey hasn't been easy. But it's been liberating, and rewarding, and for many, provided healing and deliverance.

This book is a tool that's meant to be used, this is not just another book. Each story has a common thread that ties us all together. Fear. As you go through this book, I encourage you to get excited about what God is positioning you for on the other side of your fear. Bigger and Better is HERE. Your next level has so much power attached to it, and when you arrive there…nothing will look the same. Fear will try to convince you that your problems, issues, and past are much bigger than your WIN, but fear is a liar. Stretch through the pages of this book and grow into your next season. This book will teach you resilience, it will require you to grow… and that may be uncomfortable but trust it. Trust the process and let the process position you. This is just the beginning. It is done.

With Love,
Tiana Patrice

REBIRTH

BY TYECIA POWELL

dear fear, you can't have my ...

Dear fear,

I remember a time in my life when you were the Father I did not have. You loved me, you talked to me, and you were always there. You know how everyone talks about how much little boys need their daddies? Well this little girl needed hers, and you were there. You helped mold me into a young lady who didn't feel pretty enough or smart enough; just not enough. You taught me to run, to drink, deceive people, and not trust anyone. Man, we had crazy times together. Truth be told, you were my best friend, but I had to walk away from you because you also hurt me.

You wouldn't allow me to grow, to let my light shine, and I had a lot to contribute to the world. I remember every time I used to come to you, I would be physically and mentally tired, defeated even. You know, you never once tried to help me get out of that place. You actually kept me there. I had to learn to breathe again because of you. And when I tried to leave, you sent my biological father back into my life to stir up why I needed you in the first place. Guess what, Fear. The moment you meant for evil actually transcended my life. Don't get me wrong, I considered running back to your arms. I know, I know. I even hung out with you a few times, but deep down I knew I needed something else, someone else. I needed to walk away.

The day my biological father emailed back into my life has proven to be the change agent I needed. It was my burning bush! Ok Fear, you got my full attention with that one, but because of you, I now choose to move forward to face all that has tried to break me, stop me, hinder me, and bind me. Facing my biological father meant I had to ask some hard questions, of him, of my mother, and of my grandmother. I wasn't even sure if I wanted to know the answers. You know what I learned as I started my rebirth? That moment when you let go and you're crying that ugly cry; in that moment all becomes clear. Not clear like someone writing you a letter, but clear like a mirror being turned on you and you have no choice but to look at yourself eye to eye. You have to decide in that moment to get up and go the extra mile, where the traffic is lighter, or go back to what you know and possibly never fulfill your God-given purpose.

Hey Fear, I am going the extra mile! I am choosing to live purposefully, I am building a relationship with my biological father, I am facing every challenge ahead of me with my shoulders pulled back and my chest up because you just showed me you are no good for me. While my father may have been the catalyst for my rebirth, this rebirth keeps happening. I have mended, started, and fostered relationships. I have grown in my profession, and I have raised my voice to sow love into others. I can finally say with confidence: Dear Fear, you can't have my rebirth. I will always win against you because I am doing a great work and I cannot come down.

Signed,
Tyecia Powell

You Can't Have My Rebirth

◆━━━━━━━━━━━━━━━━━━━━━◆

"What happens when the bottom falls out?" my therapist asked me three weeks into our weekly sessions. I froze, tensed up, looked out the window. I won't let the bottom fall out. "I see this makes you uncomfortable. Why?" she asked. "Beth, I have a plan A-Z. I plan for failures, for missteps." "Ty, the bottom can and will fall out. The best laid plans can often fail," she replied. A week later, I went on a two-week journey hiking through Peru and I found my answer. What happens when the bottom falls out? A rebirth.

After undergrad, I spent some time in Poughkeepsie, NY as a Grad Assistant for Marist College, but decided to come back home to Baltimore because I missed my family. That was the furthest I had ever been away from them. Eight months in Poughkeepsie was long enough. I stopped my Master's program, left my job and moved back home to Baltimore, taking a teaching job at a local high school. However, being back in Baltimore was short lived. While I had my family there, I had to leave Baltimore. Fear lived too close to me there, and I thought I could out run him by moving again. I fought leaving Baltimore. I wouldn't tell anyone what was going on with me internally. I kept to myself a lot and tried not to worry my family with my issues. Being the oldest of 5, I was built tough. I never wanted to burden my parents anymore than I had to. I had this nagging feeling that I needed something; a change, a new life, a release, anything. I moved to Georgia where my aunt and uncle lived. I hid from fear there, or at least I thought I did. But that nagging feeling returned again after five years of being in Georgia. This time I turned to my journal and devotionals for the answer, and I settled on releasing through communication. I needed to release some things that were holding me back, so I did just that. My release started with one request. "Hey little brother, do you know how I can get in touch with Pops?"

My biological father (Pops) left me when I was 2, but no worries, my Daddy filled that void. My mother remarried, and I really don't remember life without my stepdad (Daddy). Pops had two kids that I later met when I was 12. All I remember of that time is riding a plane by myself from Baltimore to Hawaii. I don't even remember much of my time there. I didn't have much communication with any of them after that initial meeting until I was 18. My uncle met up with Pops on a visit to Hawaii and told him all the great things I was doing and had achieved. The next thing I know, Pops was at my college dorm asking me to meet his father, visit his family, have dinner with him, and oh yeah, tell my mom he wanted custody of me so he could stop paying child support. Newsflash! I was 18, a legal adult. Neither of them had custody of me! Needless to say, there was silence again after that visit. I did not hear from him again. When I made the decision to reach out and Google my brother, it was quite a task. He has a very common name, and having only met him twice, I had to search pictures and various social media outlets until I found the one closest to looking something like me. Before I had a chance to reach out to Pops, my little brother must have said something to him because I got an email from him a few days later. Why did he all of a sudden get the courage to email me? What did my brother say to him to make him email now? He never thought about emailing or reaching out before. Was he trying to prove something to my brother? Did he feel obligated since my brother said something? I was supposed to be in control here. This was my battle with Fear. Anger set in and doubt creeped back into my life. But the pastor told me in a sermon the Sunday after I received that email to see past what is in front of me in order to surpass it and to give up in order to give in. My steps were ordered even as I was trying to do this on my own. I quickly learned how to lean into God and give him control. I had to make a decision to move forward, to make the next bold move. I needed God to intercede because Fear still had my number and knew my address. I needed to believe God. Period. Not just believe in Him to get me through this. I was not sure I knew how to do that yet. I went to church every Sunday after that email. I paid attention to my pastor's every word, every little nugget. He would say things like, 'The essence of following Jesus is more about self-denial not self-improvement,' or 'die to yourself, so you can say yes to God'. I would sit and write relentlessly as if writing his words would overwrite the story Fear had already written for me.

The day I got that email, I wanted to blame Pops for all the things that I have been through in my life, but people that blame things won't change things, and I know these truths like the back of my hand. I needed to change things; change me, change my position in life. I needed a rebirth, but Fear told me change was impossible. It took me 61 days to respond to Pops' email. It took 61 days for my heart and mind to reach a compromise. My heart declared war with my mind the day I opened that email. 61 days before I fully trusted God. 61 days before I lost control. 61 days. Now, I'm not into numerology, but this 61 is significant and I didn't do it on purpose. It's just how things started to reveal themselves to me as I was on my journey to a rebirth. 61 is the atomic number for Promethium, a rare radioactive metal. Fitting right? Because the sightings of my biological father were rare. The 61st word in the Bible is God, and boy, did I need God for this one.

This instance with my father began to shift the trajectory of my life. This was the start of my rebirth. At the time, I did not know it was a rebirth. I thought it was just another one of life's obstacles. It took two years after that email for me to forgive Pops with my whole heart. We met and had conversations in within that time, but a part of my rebirth required me to find forgiveness in my heart. Once I forgave him, his family was next, specifically my grandmother. They left me soon after he did. Even though they had always lived close by, they never reached out. After 17 years, I walked into a room where I was not even sure the people in there knew who I was. And as God would have it, the day I visited my grandmother, my aunt and uncle were there. "Is that Tyecia?" someone asked. Ok God, so you're going to make me do this all at once, huh? As I sat there and prayed, forgiving all of them in my heart, as Fear would have it, my grandmother said, "Don't stay away so long again." Wait, what? Forgiveness quickly left my mind and another nice little F word crept in. Me stay away? I was the child! Why did you stay away from me? I have not been back, and that's on me. Hey, I'm still on this journey. God's still working on me.

Pops being back in the picture brought up some interesting feelings about my mom as well. Sometimes, having a present parent who is also absent can be just as bad. For a child struggling with being enough, having a mother who could not accept me being a lesbian created an absence as well. Absence of seeing me, 1st kid in the family to graduate high school without being pregnant. 1st kid in the family to get a full college scholarship. A kid who never really asked for anything, but did everything. I struggled my entire life with feeling enough. Not feeling pretty enough; I do not look like my siblings. Smart enough; all my friends got better grades than me. Good enough; I was never a starter on my high school team. In order to be reborn you have to shed the old. I had to communicate again, open up, and I did. I forgave my mother with my whole heart.

This is not a story to bash my parents. They love me and there is no doubt in my mind about that, and I believe they did the best they could while struggling with their own fears. While it took me over 30 years to learn that all of what I struggled with was preparation for the journey ahead, the lessons I learned took me to dark places. I learned to build walls to protect myself from hurt. I used to chase perfection, seeking success. I chased validation from others, dating the prettiest women to feel pretty enough, and chased degrees to feel smart enough. What does ENOUGH even feel like, look like? The day I realized what a rebirth was and how God has always ordered my steps and positioned me where I needed to be, when I needed to be there, was the day I gave up. Gave up fear, gave up me. God sent my world on a downward spiral to get my full attention. I tried to buy a house. I had a plan, I had the money, I had the credit score… but the answer was NO. I tried to become an Assistant Principal. I had a plan, I took the test, I have degrees, I paid my dues, I do the work, but NO. I lost my job. FAILURE. Hello FEAR!

Like many people going through tough times, hard times, trying times, I contemplated taking my life. Why was all this happening? I felt like I was in the middle of a Solange song. I tried to drink it away, I tried to sex it away. I tried anything that would make me forget. The bottom fell out. Even the best laid plans can fail. How do you recover from all this stuff hitting you at once? I was scared to apply for jobs, afraid that my last job told them about all the nonsense that led to me losing my job. I was scared to ask for help, because Ty is supposed to be the strong one, the one that helps everyone else out. I was scared to fail, but I did. There was only a small circle of people that knew what 2016 took me through. A small group of people saw me drowning, tried to save me and I pushed them away. Yet they prayed for me. Fear held me for a long time; fear of failure, fear of being enough. Fear has been riding with me from the day my Pops left. Fear replaced my absent parent. If my own father didn't want me and my mother didn't see me, why would anyone else? Fear led me to relationship after relationship, not because I was trying to be promiscuous, but because fear told me to run from every situation that would lead me away from Him, my true father, GOD.

But God! At my lowest point, I walked into a yoga studio, attempting something I had never done before. I was just looking for an escape, and instead I found me. That class taught me to accept the grace and forgiveness of God in order to heal and be reborn. That night after class, in June 2016, I sat in the middle of my bedroom floor and cried harder than I ever cried in my life. And that night, as I surrendered, I was reborn again and it was all made clear to me. I'm doing a great work. I cannot come down. Everything in my life was a building block for what was next. From mentoring other young people to building community through my testimony. I needed to go through every challenge in my life to get to this point, get to this next, to get me to release the hold Fear had on my life. God knew I had a battle in front of me and he needed to strengthen and sharpen me for what was next. Lord, I do not know what you are doing but give me eyes to see and ears to hear so I may go, so I may say yes. Dear Fear, I am reborn. You no longer have a place in my life. What's next God?

Stop for a second, and read this next line to yourself. YOU ARE ENOUGH! Read it again out loud. Now, listen to me right now with your whole heart. You do not have to pay for the sins of your parents. You are not a product of their battles with Fear, you are a product of love. It is your job to take their lessons as lessons you do not need to repeat. At 36, I learned something I want you to learn now. Don't wait as long as I did, you are in the midst of a rebirth. When your father walks out, when your mother walks out, it is your turn to be reborn into the life they were wishing for, the life they thought they were creating but their own fears kept from them. Pack your backpack, follow me in this new journey, along this new path. I'm going to give a choice in this moment. You can choose to walk this path in my direction. Don't worry, I will walk with you, carry you if I have to. You can also choose to forge your own path, and that's ok too. I will be here cheering you on every step of the way, but I beg you not to choose their path and only use their path to get you started. Their path is your catalyst, your start of something new, something great. Sarah Jakes preached a sermon called 'Boundaries'. She urged all under the sound of her voice to respect boundaries because you have to give credit for the past and what it has accomplished, but you also have to set boundaries and disrupt boundaries. Boundaries are going to be the foundation of your rebirth. I give you permission to walk out of that caged life. The door is actually open, but no one taught you how to open the latch. I'm opening the latch for you, I am giving you an opening. Walk through, crawl through, jump through, pull yourself through if you need to. Your absent parent is not the end of your story, it's the beginning.

A rebirth requires you not to just see yourself at mile one, but to see yourself at mile 12 finishing. What's at mile 12, waiting for you, that you are letting Fear keep you from?

_____

_____

_____

_____

Perfection happens in motion, while at work. You cannot perfect anything without releasing it. Make a decision to move forward with your great work today. What's your next BOLD move?

_____

_____

_____

_____

LEGACY

BY TYWAUNA WILSON

dear fear, you can't have my ...

Dear fear,

Get off my line! I am not taking anymore of your crazy messages! You whispered you can't, you won't, you're not, for far too long. You painted the picture that I couldn't be a phenomenal woman because I came from a "disadvantaged background," where statistics said if I became somebody, I was one of the lucky ones. Fear, you are a trip! You tried to make my family legacy out to be something I shouldn't be proud of because of our imperfect picture. If it wasn't for my history, I know I wouldn't be the woman I am today. Sure, life had its challenges growing up in a single parent low-income household. And yeah, I would have liked to grow up being daddy's little girl, but not having a storybook childhood is no reason for you to try to make me feel less than. Fear, it seems like you always know when to strike. When I get the confidence to be bold, brave, follow my dreams and trust the process, you conveniently call or leave a message of self-doubt and defeat. Ring, ring...this is Fear calling. I know you think you are going to be somebody special, but don't forget the first man that should have validated you wasn't even available to sign off on your very existence. So how special can you be? There you go bringing up old stuff.

For a long time, your messy tactics of recycling past hurts had me caught up in a tailspin. You know how to show up at all the right times to try to distract me from the promises God has for my life. Well Fear, I've had enough! My God told me to ride with him and he will ride with me, so I am picking up my legacy and moving forward, full speed ahead. I know that you can only turn those challenging parts of my story into speed bumps if I give you access to my heart and mind. My desire and persistence to achieve all that is destined for me is far greater than any distraction you can send my way. I know it doesn't matter how you start, but how you finish. My humble beginnings created the strong foundation on which I stand. So today, I boldly say to you, Fear, You can't have my legacy! It's worth fighting for. I represent the many voices that will never be heard and faces that will never be seen. I know I can, I will, and I am the voice this world needs to be transformed. And there is nothing you can do about it.

Signed, a phenomenal woman.
-Coach Tee Wilson

You Can't Have My Legacy

"Your story is the greatest legacy that you will leave to your friends. It's the longest-lasting legacy you will leave to your heirs."
~Steve Sain

"Kids that are raised by single mothers are disadvantaged. You're going to have daddy issues. How do you think you are going to go to college when your parents didn't even complete high school? You're going to have to try really hard to overcome your background. If you do become successful, you're one of the lucky ones."

Fear, I give it to you. You are clever with your thoughts. You know how to add just a little bit of truth to your statements to make them believable. You worked very hard to convince me that a young brown-skinned skinny girl with buck teeth and a crazy hairdo from Dayton, Ohio would never be good enough, pretty enough, or smart enough to be a real difference maker in this world. Sure, my upbringing wasn't traditional with a mom, dad, and a white picket fence, but it was very similar to that of many of the people I knew. When my mom was a teenager, she got pregnant by a smooth brother from Cleveland who was absent for most of my early years. Not having a dad in the home was pretty common, so I didn't consider that a disadvantage. I grew up during a time when drugs were plaguing most of the families in my community. Mine was no exception. I am not sure who came up with illegal drugs and why, but they were evil! The lies, the hurt, and the craziness that ensued from them was unbelievable.

Lucky for me, while a lot of my family and community were being destroyed by the great white rock, my granny was not involved in those shenanigans. I spent a lot of time with her when I was younger, especially when my mom had to work. She provided a consistent life and made sure that I went to school every day. I loved hanging with my granny, except for when I heard her being physically and verbally abused. I never understood how someone could hurt the person they claimed to love. I didn't really know what a man's love was like growing up since I didn't grow up with my dad, but I knew for sure that if a man's love came in the form of abuse, I wasn't interested. I did finally connect with my dad when I was around thirteen, and I was so excited. I was looking forward to being daddy's little girl, but I have to admit I was kind of afraid. I hoped we would make up for lost time, but was that even possible after he had already missed so much? Fear tried to plant thoughts of anger and bitterness for the missed moments, but I was determined to make the best out of the time we did have. With all of these hindrances that life's hand dealt me, would it be possible for this world to take me seriously? Would I grow bitter and angry? Could I overcome this? Are there lessons to be learned from my family dynamics or should I be ashamed and lose my legacy?

Lessons Learned from the Unlikely Experts
"Your family legacy doesn't define who you are destined to become, instead it strengthens the story you will leave behind for others to be enriched by it." ~Coach Tee Wilson

You can't pick your family or the circumstances you are born into. You got what you got and there are lessons to be learned from every situation. God knew what He was doing even before you came into existence, and He placed just the right people in your family to teach you a lesson. You can spend a lifetime giving energy and focus on the unfortunate parts of your story or you can use the lemons you have to make lemonade.

Although my mom, dad, and granny didn't have a formal education and life presented its own challenges and hardships, their legacies intertwined on my life inspired my success. I always remember them saying that if you are smart, you will be able to do anything. So, I made school my lemonade. Through all of the distractions happening in the background, getting an education was always constant. Reading allowed me to go to new places, writing allowed me to be whomever I wanted to be, math allowed me to be able to count the millions I hoped to make one day, and science; well, I just liked science. Fear, you thought the negative talk would stop me, but it gave me energy to keep dreaming!

Lessons and Values from my Mom
"If you have faith the size of a mustard seed and utilize the tools you have been given to your advantage, anything is possible."
~Mom

My mom taught me lessons in having faith and leveraging resources. She always told me to work smarter, not harder and to use my head. My mom and I went through a lot together growing up, but she remained faithful that it would work out in the end. Even during the time that we didn't have a place of our own to call home, she was able to see the silver lining and make the situation work. It's easy to be faithful when things are going right, but it takes true faith to endure when things are not going well. My mom was an example of that. She was always finding resources. When I was 13, my mom found a program that granted me my first summer job as a camp counselor, instilling a strong work ethic. In middle school, she found a summer program at Ohio State University that instilled independence. I guess that is where the work smart, not hard message came in. In high school, my mom found an opportunity for me to experience my first educational trip and plane ride that instilled courage. When it was time for me to go off to college, my mom jumped on the highway (This was her kicking fear in the butt. Highway driving terrified her!) and drove me 2 ½ hours to Kentucky State University, which instilled determination and excellence. We never knew how it would all come to pass, but my mom believed and just knew it would. A strong belief in a higher being has been key in making my life complete.

Lessons and Values from my Dad
"Everyone needs to have multiple streams of income. Don't wait for someone to make it possible for you. Create your own opportunities. It's ok to do something never seen before."
~Dad

My dad taught me lessons in innovation and entrepreneurship. We didn't spend a lot of time together before he passed in 2014, but the tools he left me with are more impactful at this point in my life than ever before. It's ironic that the very person who wasn't around to validate me at birth, left me with all the resources needed to be an independent phenomenal woman who knows how to get her coins. I can remember my dad telling me he could make more money with his businesses than I could make with a degree. He told me not to get comfortable working for someone. "Make your own money," he said. At the time, I thought he was crazy because there was no way his hustle could outweigh my formal education. My dad always had numerous investments, including real estate property, food trucks (he had food trucks in the 1990s, before they were popular), after hours clubs, and a car wash that is still open to this day. Little did I know, this was setting the foundation for me to "make my own money" and creating generational wealth. Being innovative and having an entrepreneurial spirit has always been in my genes, even when fear tried to tell me it wasn't and that owning my own business wasn't possible. In 2017, I kicked fear in the butt and gave breath to my leadership training and coaching company, Trendy Elite, LLC!

Lessons and Values from my Granny

"Leadership is not about titles or qualifications. God calls people of all backgrounds to lead, you only have to have a desire and will to serve."
~Granny

My granny taught me lessons in leadership and the importance of volunteerism. Even though my granny was a homemaker for most of her life, she always valued leading and giving to others. My granny instilled leadership through her involvement in the Ladies Auxiliary, where she served as the President for many years. She organized several community service programs and raised money for veterans during her tenure. Participating in the Ladies Auxiliary was her outlet to escape her own reality and help others, even though she needed help herself. Little did I know, she was setting the foundation for me to seek leadership roles and give to others regardless of what is happening in my life. I credit my granny's involvement in the Ladies Auxiliary to leading me to become a member of Delta Sigma Theta Sorority, Inc, where I have served in several leadership roles, participated in activities that benefited the community, and raised funds to benefit the lives of others.

The Present

"There is a lesson in every legacy. It's those parts that make us our best. Fear will try to kill, steal, destroy and discredit those parts that makes you who you are. Tell Fear to push on, you're fighting for yours! It's your legacy and it's yours to keep."
~ Coach Tee Wilson

When I think back on my legacy, I realize fear wanted me to be ashamed. Fear wanted me to be silent and keep my story to myself. I don't think so! There is a lesson to be learned in all stories, and my untraditional background taught me that it doesn't matter where you come from. If you know where you want to go, God will provide a road for you to get there. There may be other young girls wondering if their family legacy will be the downfall of their future. I am here as a witness to say, it will only be your downfall if you let it. There is a lesson to be learned in every situation and from those closest to you.

Everything that was perceived as disadvantageous propelled me to greater heights. Everything that was meant for me to have, I have been blessed with. I never thought I would get married, but I have been able to find love and marry my best friend who loves and adores me. Nobody in my family had ever gone to college. I not only went to college, but graduated with three degrees including a graduate degree. I was picked on and made to feel I wasn't good enough, but I have received recognition & distinction as a top forty under 40 in my community and profession, which has also given me the opportunity to teach leaders and scientists around the globe. I didn't come from a legacy of family working in high profile careers, yet I currently serve as the System Chemistry Director for a regional clinical laboratory within a major healthcare system. Through my business, I transform the lives of many leaders near and far. The impossible is possible when you step on fear and keep walking. This is only the beginning of my story, the rest is still unfolding. Everyone has a best seller waiting to be written. Thanks for reading a snippet of mine!

What parts of your story are you hiding or afraid to share because you think others will judge you?

_____

_____

_____

_____

What value did your family legacy leave you with that transformed you into the person you are today?

_____

_____

_____

_____

Your story is your legacy. What message will you leave for the next generation?

_____

_____

_____

_____

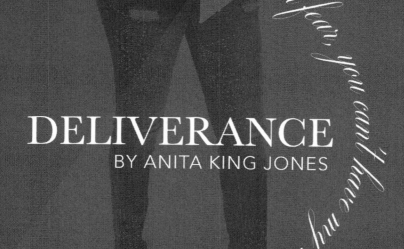

DELIVERANCE

BY ANITA KING JONES

dear fear, you can't have my ...

Dear fear,

So many times you have continuously reminded me of all my past mistakes. You were there when I experienced one failed marriage after another. Fear, you tricked me into believing that my mental and physical abuse was part of me becoming submissive. That was a lie. The more I submitted, the more my heart was trampled on. I was worth more than you gave me credit. I just wanted to be loved without all the dramatics. But I have to admit, after each fall, God picked me up, dusted me off and gave me the strength and courage to try again. I must take this time out to say thank you, Fear, for the intricate part you played in my struggles and doubt which ultimately caused me to grow in the Lord and pursue my true purpose from God. No longer will you hold me back from doing the things Christ has commissioned me to do. I will soar like an eagle with my wings mounted up high. Fear, you have caused me to put ALL my trust in God and believe and know that His word is true. He is a strong deliverer. Psalm 34:19 reminds me that the righteous will have many afflictions, but God will deliver me from them all. God has shown me that I was created to uplift and inspire, exhort and encourage, and then reach back and pull forward those have had the life beaten out of them "in the name of love." He has also shown me that NO weapon formed against me shall prosper. No longer will I be bound in any area of my life because God has set me free. In this season, God showed me that He has all power and can break any yoke which tries to keep me bound. Thank you, Fear, for pushing me into the purpose of transforming lives. I will no longer sit back quietly but I declare by the power of God's anointing, I will touch hearts to break the yoke of bondage in the lives of others.

Goodbye forever,
Anita King Jones

You Can't Have My Deliverance

◆─────────────────────────────◆

After experiencing a power outage caused by the storm, I went to a girlfriend's house for a couple of hours. When I returned home, he questioned me with a knife down by his side. He asked where I had been. I told him exactly where I was and that he could call her to verify it. I was accused of lying and being with another man. As his voice got louder, my tone softened. The Holy Spirit instructed me to psychologically talk him out of killing me, right there in my bedroom, by telling him things he wanted to hear. His son overheard him screaming at me and came to my rescue. This created a major altercation which led to him trying to stab his own son for protecting me. The turning point was when he told the officer that he was going to kill me and himself. Life had become a recurring cycle. I was trying to be God to someone who didn't care enough about themselves nor me. I don't have the power to save anyone. You must want to be saved. I had to break the cycle. People will continue to do to you only what you allow them to.

I am reminded of John 5:6, "Wilt thou be made whole?" When God said Yoke Breaking, I immediately knew why. It represents the need to be freed, maybe from enslavement or subjection to another person as well as oppression and suffering. Breaking the yoke shows liberation from bondage, oppression, and exploitation. Regardless of what God said, I almost didn't write my story. The Lord released me about 7 years ago. God said it is finished. No longer did I have to suffer through an abusive marriage. I started writing, but I was overwhelmed by all that

God had brought me through. Some of the details brought back so many emotions I had to close the book. God kept opening it back up to complete the work He started in me. I tried to testify about some other life changing experience God had brought me through. No matter how much I tried to change this story, God brought me right back to this ugly truth. It absolutely terrified me to see all of this on paper. It took me back to a dark place that I really never wanted to revisit. God brought me through a horrible experience that some women never make it out of. In that season, I discovered that God is able and willing to deliver us and break every yoke that may have us bound if WE allow Him to. I was created to impact lives and encourage others because I have become an overcomer. I can exhort and help encourage those who Satan tries to steal joy from. A life might be lost if I don't tell my story. Jesus might not get introduced to somebody if I fail to say what God told me to say. My testimony can bear witness of the miracles of God. This can help someone else that might be going through.

God taught me to stop being a victim and become victorious. I know this sounds naïve, but I just want to be loved unconditionally. I deserve to be loved with all of my flaws. Is there anyone out there that can just love me for who I am and what I stand for? I have experienced one bad marriage after another. I only wish I had consulted God in my decision before I said "I do." Even when God said 'Not now,' I questioned if that was His voice but, I continued on with it anyway. So when all hell broke loose within the first year, I could only blame myself. I was in a marriage for 18 years to a man that claimed he loved me. I guess he thought he was Solomon which would have allowed him to have wives and many concubines. What he really had was an obsession for me and thought I was his property. I left him several times for having affairs and other abusive behavior. Eighteen years later, there I was broke, busted and trying to recoup from the all the lies, all the cheating and all that he took from me. Oh, but how can I forget? He did leave me some things, things that I almost couldn't get rid of even with the strongest antibiotics. He also promised if I got a protective order against him, he would kill me and kill himself. I was afraid to stay but also afraid to leave. I should have listened to that still small voice when God said, "No, not now." It almost cost me my life. We must be patient and be sure of the voice of the Lord. The only way to become sure is to enter into relationship with God first, before you say 'I do.'

They say the apple doesn't fall far from the tree. My parents were married over 50 years. They also say you are a product of your environment. My mom was a devout Christian that made me nervous, talking to strangers about Jesus any and everywhere we went. She was embarrassingly submissive to my dad. He always thought he had to have the last say. Still, my mom lived life victoriously and was blessed by her obedience to God. Although I didn't agree with all that I saw, I started to accept similar behavior from men. I found myself saying I want to be like my mom when I grow up. I received the anointed legacy my mom left to carry on. Be careful what you ask for.

Never underestimate the power to take your life in another direction. I had to change the way I was thinking. I quickly discovered I had to trust and know that God could fix it for me and through me. I had to choose life or death. Satan uses fear to fill our heads and hearts with doubt and remind us of our weaknesses. He tells us that we are nothing and will never be anything. He makes us think we can never make it out of our circumstances. There comes a time when you have to totally submit it all into the hands of God. Let him have the problem and don't take it back. I want the world to know that we must trust in the Lord with ALL our heart, lean not to your own understanding. If we acknowledge Him, he will direct us. We must learn to live like we trust God with all things big and small. God can carry you when you think you can't go any further. God has a way of removing things that are not for you so that you can get to what he has prepared for you. There is nothing too hard for God if you would only believe, trust and obey.

I also came to the conclusion that all that I have gone through was necessary. You become stronger with every storm you face. Fear tried to shut me down and shut my mouth. People who had gone through the same thing were judging me and expecting me to react differently because I was a preacher. They expected me to be God, stay and save myself. I isolated myself and didn't think I was worthy to even worship God. Question after question formulated in my head. How on earth would I ever be able to start over? How would I go on since I had never been unemployed? I also felt lonely and rejected. After 35 years, I felt forced to leave all of my friends, family and church. I had to decide what to do next. I was afraid of the unknown and I felt ashamed. What would those who know me think about me? I preached forgiveness and reconciliation, but I wasn't practicing it. I did not feel worthy to encourage anyone else since I had failed relationship after relationship. I sat in a season of silence.

I wouldn't proclaim God's word, although I had accepted the call. I was afraid to move on. As a woman of God, I felt like I was setting a bad example by leaving. It took me a while to learn to trust myself with the business of God again.

But when I came to myself, I knew all that I went through in life was necessary to bring me into my purpose. God showed me there are many who are physically and mentally abused that don't know which way to turn. My worship and praise became important in my time of trouble. I had to put aside all shame, guilt and fear and praise God like I had lost my mind. I decided to worship God although my change had not yet manifested itself. I stop asking 'why me' and started asking God 'what would you have me to say today.' God showed me that my life would break yokes of bondage and deliver someone else that was going through. Trials come to make us stronger. Each victory brings us into our purpose and destiny in Christ. All of this taught me to trust in the Lord with ALL my heart and lean not to my own understanding. Consult God with all things. I had to totally rely on God's direction and covering in this season. I discovered that I didn't need to, nor did I have the ability to fix everything because God was there waiting for me to acknowledge that He was an able God and that I needed Him. The more I prayed and leaned on God, I found that I was not alone. The Holy Spirit was there to comfort me. God was able to heal my broken heart when I cried out to Him. God hears and answers prayers. There comes a time when you have to participate in your healing and blessing and just know that what you go through is necessary to process you into your purpose.

God has more power than my problems and He has prepared me for a life of purpose. He has proven to be my protector and my guide, if I would just listen and obey. I have a passion to see struggling women free in their minds and spirits. God want us to be about His business, not allowing anyone to keep us oppressed and afraid. God commissioned me to reach the lost and to tell my story as a testimony of His faithfulness, His goodness, His mercy and His grace. I feel like I am running a race of faith. We must listen to God's voice telling us what to do next. Sometimes God whispers, but sometimes He has to scream at the top of his lungs, throwing roadblocks in front of us because we refuse to listen. God is always speaking, whether it is through His word, through prayers, through other believers, or even through our circumstances. Was I even listening?

I learned some things on this journey. You are not defined by what people say you are. We must recognize who we belong to. You are a child of the King. I learned to love myself and now others can love me. It is important to develop a relationship with God so you can clearly know His voice. We are not alone and He promises never to leave us nor forsake us. Put your faith and trust in God and let Him lead the way. Totally trust God with His purpose for your life. God is the only one who can heal your broken spirit and restore your joy. You must learn to delight yourself in the Lord and He will give you the desires of your heart. Worship and praise God as if He has already done what you asked and speak it into existence. God also showed me that a delay is not always a denial. Thank God His faithfulness does not in any way depend on our faithfulness. God can make a way in the desert. He can make a way out of no way.

God can also restore to you all that Satan tried to steal from you. God restored me and gave me a blessing that I never thought I was worthy to receive. God is amazing. Trust and believe in Him with all your heart. I encourage you to allow God to complete the work He started in you until He says it is finished. Continue to press toward the mark.

Discuss a time that you were able to serve someone based on God's deliverance in your life.

_____

_____

_____

_____

What are some things God has used to process you into his purpose? Explain.

_____

_____

_____

_____

POWER

BY ASHLEY LITTLE

dear fear, you can't have my... fear, you can't have my...

Dear fear,

I will not let you distract me from my destiny. You have tried to stop my journey by sending distractions. No longer will I allow you to do that. Fear, you can't have my focus. You can't have my talents and my gifts. You wanted me to be intimidated and not step out on faith. Fear, you sent people into my life disguised as friends to distract me. Fear, you can't control me.

Fear, you wanted me to be afraid to share what God has done in my life. You wanted me to be afraid of what people might say or think of me. Fear, you can't stop what God is doing in my life. What God has for me is for me. What people think of me is none of my business. Fear, you wanted me to remain silent and not speak up. I'm not afraid to voice my opinion.

Fear, you wanted me to remain captive in relationships that were hurting me. You will not have my heart and I will walk away. Fear, you tried to use death to discourage me. Fear, I am strong. You wanted me to remain silent when I was discriminated against in the workplace because of the color of my skin. Fear, I will not remain silent and I will stand up for myself.

Fear, you wanted me to miss my blessings and not take promotions because you thought I was too young. You can't stop what God has for me, age doesn't matter. Fear, you tried to bully me at a young age because you knew I had special talents and gifts. You can't stop me from being successful.

Fear, you sent people in my life disguised as support to distract me from my goals. I am smart and I have discernment. I will encourage myself. Fear, you tried to stop me from writing my letter. Guess what fear, it is written. Fear, you thought you were going to keep me from my destiny because you knew I was a leader. You tried to discourage, attack, and gossip about me. Fear, you didn't know I was a seed. I'm going to the next level and I'm leaving you behind. I will reach my destiny. You haven't seen nothing yet. New chapter, new beginning, new season, and I will embrace every moment. I'm not even close to my peak. Fear, I serve notice on you today...

Goodbye,
Ashley Little

You Can't Have My Power

I remember a time when fear tried to make an ugly appearance in my life. It was May 2011, and my world was coming to an end when I lost my grandfather. He was wise, God-fearing, well-respected, loving, caring, giving, protective, and he loved his family. He was the glue of my family. When he left, we were devastated. During that time, I was depressed and unhappy, my heart was broken. He was my friend, my support system, my biggest fan and my prayer warrior. There were times when I fought myself about moving away from my family because of my career. I wanted more time with my grandfather and I felt like my career got in the way of that. Fear tried to discourage me by making me feel bad about stepping out on faith and chasing my dreams. Fear tried to use my grandfather to distract me and make me lose focus. My grandfather was my biggest fan and he wanted me to chase my dreams and never give up. God wanted me to depend on him for my every need. Losing my grandfather has helped me overcome my fear of death and has taught me to cherish life. My sister, life will throw you curveballs and God will wreck all your plans to get your attention. He wants us to grow and depend on him. Does God have your attention? Are you afraid of losing someone close to you?

In 2015, my dad was diagnosed with cancer. It was one of the hardest years of my life. I thought my life was falling apart. I was sad, depressed and I didn't want to talk to anyone. I thought my dad was leaving us, and I was angry because he didn't tell us he was sick. Fear wanted me to be upset with my father and to feel like he didn't care enough about his family to tell us this horrible news. Fear knew how important family is to me and wanted me to be afraid to talk about it. I felt like a knife had stabbed me in my heart because I didn't want to go through this again. I lost my grandfather to cancer, and I was not going to let cancer take my father. Fear tried to test my faith by using my father's sickness. I was determined to fight for my father and to keep him encouraged. I prayed every day against cancer. I told myself everyday that my father does not have cancer and he was going to make it through. I knew this was a test of faith and I had to speak life no matter the circumstances. Fear wanted me to give up on my dad and accept it, but God had a different agenda. God took me through those moments to test my faith and grow my relationship with him. He wanted me to be able to share my story to encourage someone else who may have been going through the same storm. I am thankful, blessed, and proud to say that my father made it through the storm and he is cancer free! I learned that sometimes when you go through storms they are not for you, they are for someone else. I believe God used my father to get my attention and bring me closer to him. I learned to cherish every moment and that tomorrow is not promised; to speak life, even when the road is dark and to always push through and fight. Always remember, our storms develop and shape us into the person we are today. Storms are good for us to go through because they keeps us humble and will always teach us something. Life is full of learning experiences, so remember to always remain a student. What storms did you have to endure? How did you feel? Did you give up or did you fight? My journey throughout life has not always been open to the public eye. I am a very private person, but I had to learn to embrace and share my journey so I can help someone else along the way. The turning point in my life was when I lost my grandfather. It was the first time I lost someone who meant the world to me. The fear of dying was always scary until I lost my grandfather. I learned to always put God first, live a fulfilling life, break barriers and take risks. Also, to live with no regrets and to live everyday as if it was my last. I challenge you, my sister, to enjoy the journey of life and cherish every moment. Are you enjoying the journey? Are you living your best life?

FEAR, you have no power. I am EVICTING you! You are not welcome and you are not allowed in my life. I'm an energetic, God-fearing, ambitious, smart, educated, talented, career-driven, strong, determined, classy risk-taker, go-getter, successful woman from a small town called Wadesboro, North Carolina. My family believed in God, family, education and going against the grain. I grew up in a very loving and supportive household and I was always taught to never give up, no matter what life throws at me. I was always determined to be successful and I was not going to let anyone or anything stop me. Throughout my life, I have had many great experiences that have shaped me into the person I am today. Growing up, I was very involved in church, the community, extracurricular activities and I excelled academically throughout high school and college. Attending North Carolina A&T State University in Greensboro, North Carolina had a major impact on my life. I learned about life and stretching myself outside my comfort zone. Attending one of the top HBCUs in the country taught me how to stay focused, break barriers, take a stand and fight, develop healthy and lasting relationships, networking and public speaking skills, and to always work hard. I am thankful for my family, mentors, and friends who have encouraged me along the way.

Traveling across the world, moving from state to state for my career has been life-changing and I am thankful for every opportunity God has blessed me with. Fear wanted me to be complacent and not step out on faith. Fear wanted me to be scared of breaking barriers and to not have a voice. I would walk into rooms where I was the only black female and feel like I was not accepted because of the color of my skin. I experienced discrimination in the workplace because "they" thought I was too young. I worked in environments with people who wore many different masks and were having private meetings about me, trying to get me terminated. Who cares what "THEY" think? Favor ain't fair. Fear wanted me to give up and not stand up for myself. Fear wanted me to feel discouraged and rejected. I often ask myself, Is it because I am a strong black woman who is determined to be successful? Or, Is it because I was making people feel uncomfortable because it wasn't normal for a black woman my age to hold Executive Leadership positions? I told fear, "Age ain't nothing but a number." God has plans for my life and their opinions are none of my business. God qualifies the call, and because he put me in the positions "THEY" can't move me. My sister, don't let "THEIR" opinions stop you from being successful. Always work ten times harder and take risks. Speak up for yourself and never let anyone silence you into thinking your opinion doesn't matter. Ignore the chatter and stay focused, new levels will always bring new devils. Always remember you have a VOICE and stand up for what is right. Are you going to take the promotion? Are you going to let "THEM" stop you? Are you going to remain silent?

I lost friendships and relationships that I thought were good for me, finding out later I was wrong. I trusted and supported people who were preying on my downfall. I went through different emotions, feeling betrayed and not supported by the same people I supported along the way. I experienced friendships and roadblocks that were only distractions trying to keep me from destiny. Fear tried to stop my destiny at a young age when I was a victim of bullying in elementary school. Fear tried to discourage me by wanting me to believe I was not good enough and I had to depend on people for acceptance. Those moments did not feel good at all, and at times I felt like I had to be someone else in order to be accepted. Also, I felt like I wasn't good enough and I often asked myself, Why is this happening to me? I learned that hurt people, hurt people and to block out all of the distractions. Fear wanted me to give up and not be successful, but God had other plans for me. I experienced verbal abuse thinking he was the one, and that I should compromise and settle. I was afraid to speak up out of fear of losing him. Deep in my heart, I knew he wasn't the one but I would try to convince myself over and over again that he was. Fear wanted me to stay in a relationship that was hurting me mentally and emotionally. Fear wanted me to think I didn't deserve better. Fear wanted me to be afraid of being alone. God said, "NO! You are my daughter and I have someone better for you. I am not an author of confusion. He is not the one." Soul ties had to be broken from my life from people who should have never been connected to me. Those people were never part of my journey. Fear tried to paint a different picture in my head, making me feel like it was wrong to let those people and relationships go. Fear wanted me to compromise and settle in relationships that were hurting me and pulling me away from God and my destiny. Fear, it's over. I'm done! The mask has been revealed and I'm not going to miss my destiny. I'm a firm believer that the people you are connected to will have a major impact on your destiny. I learned that everyone is not going to support you or clap for you. You have to encourage yourself and speak life. I learned that people will disappoint and hurt you, but God will always be there. My sister, who do you need to let go of? Do you have a soul tie?

I'm very passionate about continuing to excel in my career and being able to change people's lives through education. Also, I am very passionate about mentoring, coaching, and helping people succeed in every area of their life. I believe in giving back to the people who have helped me along the way and the community that raised me. Furthermore, I believe in creating scholarships and resources to help our youth and women all over the world. My destiny motivates me every day. I am determined to go against the normal and create a legacy for my future family and future children's families. What motivates you? What is your "WHY?"

Lastly, ignoring the distractions, ignoring the negativity, encouraging myself, praying until something happens and not expecting everyone to support me has taught me some very valuable life lessons. Sis, I'm not perfect and you are not either, but please do not let your past determine your future. Everyday is a fresh new beginning to create the life you want to live. We all have a story and we all have skeletons in our closet. I encourage you today to step out on faith and be uncomfortable. I have learned along the way that being uncomfortable is a good thing because it means you are growing. This is for the woman who never gave up despite the bricks life threw at her. She was willing to take risks, be uncomfortable, and step out on faith.

What risks have you taken?

_____

_____

_____

_____

What are you willing to do to be uncomfortable?

_____

_____

_____

_____

COMING BACK

BY YVONNE CHIEDZA.-MTENGWA

dear fear, i am not ...

Dear fear,

I shudder at the thought of where I would be today, had I let you have further reign over my life. I let you take resident as far back as I could remember, listening to your whispers that convinced me I wasn't good enough, pretty enough, nor strong enough to amount to anything. As a little girl you want to be told all these things; that you are clever, you are precious, that you are cute. To be fair, mom and dad did everything to ensure that I grew into a confident young woman ready to take on the world. I had it good coming up and boasted the successes of any ambitious little girl. I'm not sure what entry point you took advantage of and at what stage in my formative years you stealthily made your landing, bringing along your friends Doubt and Insecurity. You had plans for my demise, but you see, GOD had me in the palm of His hand.

My letter to you is not about letting you in on how much you battered me in the past, because let's face it; you already know this! You already know how much time you took away from me, sprinkling fertilizer to help germinate a sense of gloom and negativity that had taken root in my life. You already know how much you choked out my previously strong sense of intelligence, self-worth and self-love; ravaging me with confusion concerning my identity in Christ and who I was born to be. You cloaked me in shame, keeping the light within an ailing flicker that fought valiantly against a cold draft of life's disappointments. It's as if you knew what I was capable of if I were free from you, and so you remained persistent, unrelenting and out to finish me; calculatingly, systematically.

As a resident of my heart and mind for so long, I imagined you, Fear, would at least land softened blows to the messy heartbreaks, and raise my head to combat the unexpected jealous-driven attacks from people I thought were my friends. But no! You made it worse, spiraling me into a deep chasm of anger and putrid self-loathing.

I could go on and on about how it hurt to experience your suffocating grip, a grip you oftentimes camouflaged as a hug, yet not of love but of self-pity. But see Fear, I won't do that today. No. I won't do that today or ever. Not anymore! I've already done enough talking in the preceding paragraphs and was done negotiating with you when I finally realised that you were bent on destroying me! I will not give you anymore airplay on this great network of success that GOD Himself has been so gracious to set up for me. I, as well as other sisters who have mustered the courage to break out from your clasps, have so much more we can talk about on this GOD-ordained station, and fear isn't one of the topics that they or I have in mind. You were exposed as recently as a few years ago for me. Your slithering attempts to make a comeback in my life are not welcome here, because GOD! You tried it again just recently when sickness knocked on my door unexpectedly. But you see, GOD keeps me and has reminded me--countless times--not to be afraid through His uncontested Word! Revelation has taught me that Fear and

FAITH cannot share living quarters, for one will surely defeat the other. It took me long enough to see this, but my heart sings with gratitude for having understood that you are powerless if I shut your words out.

Fear, I want you to know that I am not coming back to that dungeon of an existence you kept me in for so many years. I chose to confront you head on then, and I maintain my continued stance to keep fighting your methods with a full artillery of faith, anchored in prayer. I'm here to reassert my commitment to maintaining my current status-quo – doing life fearlessly and shutting you out when you enter my space with unwelcome suggestions, opinions or recommendations. Faith took over and has been an unmatched tenant thus far. I've made Faith a comfortable abode within my spirit, heart and mind and we are doing just fine figuring life out together without your interruptions.

Dear Fear, I'm not coming back! Today, and every day moving forward, I deliberately choose FAITH, anchored by prayer, hope and love. There is no room here for your disruptive nature. Oh, and don't think I forgot about your friends Doubt and Insecurity either. I've been addressing those two with the same tenacity required to keep you out of my life!

With intentions to keep you barricaded out of my heart, mind and body,
Yvonne C. Mtengwa

I'm Not Coming Back

◆━━━━━━━━━━━━━━━━━━━━━━━━━━━━━◆

"God is our refuge and strength,
an ever-present help in trouble.
2 Therefore we will not fear, though the earth give way
and the mountains fall into the heart of the sea,
3 though its waters roar and foam
and the mountains quake with their surging"
-Psalm 46:1-3

"It looks like a mass, Miss Yvonne. A mass on your left ovary," she said, staring at the screen of the ultrasound machine, "I don't want to say anything more until we run a biopsy and a few more tests to ascertain what sort of mass it is."

Silence. Deafening silence.

I sat in the doctor's office for the fourth time that week after having undergone a series of ultrasounds and MRI scans. If you've ever had to endure the clanging noise of an MRI scan and those painfully long 40-60 minutes where you aren't allowed to move, you'll understand how exhausted I was. The doctor's words came after my third rodeo with an MRI machine, and hers was the second opinion I received after leaving one hospital and coming to this one, heeding the voice of the Holy Spirit. I wanted to collapse under the weight of the words of this sweet-spirited gynecologist seated across the table from me, but I was numb.

I could tell her heart was broken. All through the week we had spoken about my kids. About how young they were, life as a working Zimbabwean mother living in the United Arab Emirates, how it compared to my season as an immigrant in America years before, the ongoing adjustments and cultural adaptations of living away from our home countries, and how stressful my job was in navigating the joys and perils of corporate communications and public relations. We had gotten to know each other quite well that week, and so understandably, she wanted to reach over and give me a hug. The mother in her so desperately wanted to tell me not to worry and that everything would be okay, but she held back. It was almost as if she knew I would breakdown – right there in her office – uncontrollably and inconsolably, and she wouldn't know what to do with me.

Fear Makes an Unwelcome Comeback

"So what does this mean?" I asked her, choking back tears but losing the battle. Within seconds my cheeks were wet with tears as I thought of those babies I had spoken so much about. What about my husband? My mom, dad? My awesome team of girlfriends and the younger siblings I hadn't seen in years. Cancer? No way! All of a sudden, I became consumed by a deep sense of trepidation, an emotion I hadn't felt in a very long time. Being told I was possibly facing cancer took me back to that place of confusion and hopelessness. It felt as though my life completely fell apart in a matter of seconds, taking me back to a fearful state I had worked so hard to get away from. So you understand the depth of what I felt in that moment and how far I have come as I share my story, allow me to give a little background to how far along I've come.

More than a decade earlier, I had started to exhibit signs of depression, having been rudely awakened to the realities of living a life in America with a lackluster commitment to spiritual growth and the pursuit of a real relationship with GOD. To combat the darkness that resided within, I had taken to consuming copious amounts of alcohol, drinking up a bottle--sometimes more, of wine after working double shifts at my not-so-great jobs. In the beginning of 2003, on a date I choose not to remember, I sat in my car in the parking lot of a gas station on Atlanta's Roswell Road, opened a bottle of painkillers nestled in my sweaty palms and downed its contents with orange juice as the chaser. I survived, and can still remember the taste of tar being pumped into my stomach to save me from the debilitating and almost fatal impact of medicinal poisoning.

On December 4th 2004, a year and a half after the "gas station incident," I was driving home, also on Roswell Road, when I was involved in a near fatal car crash that left me with a fractured pelvis and lower back, a few broken bones and the task of learning to walk again. By the sheer grace of GOD, I survived that too. You see, my life had been a rehabilitation project since then, chiseling away at the wall of fear that had ravaged me throughout my bouts with depression. After realizing that I couldn't carry on like this anymore, I had thrown overthought and caution to the wind, surrendered my life fully to Christ and asked GOD to fix me. I knew what it was to be broken, to see no end in sight and living a life choked up by thorns and thistles. And so, to be told I was possibly facing cancer was a blow to all the hard work I felt GOD helped me with in overcoming what I considered to be my issues. Sitting in that doctor's office, my whole life flashed before me; quite literally everything that had happened over the years, and I struggled to reconcile it all.

A Journey into the Origins of Depression

How had I even ended up in America anyway, having enjoyed a healthy upbringing. I lived in a good neighborhood, attended the best schools and enjoyed the sprawling backyard and pool in the often described "leafy suburbs" of Harare, Zimbabwe. Going to school in America or the United Kingdom was the dream for most in my generation, a goal I set my heart on as young as 12 years of age. While this became a reality in the summer of 2000, my enjoyment was short-lived when I had to drop out of Emory University after my father unexpectedly lost in job in the latter part of 2001.

2002 to 2007 would forever be etched in my mind as a time I fought through life fearfully. Having dropped out of college meant living and working as an illegal immigrant and juggling 1-2 jobs, working for anyone that that would allow me to without asking about my residency status. I missed my family and the comforts of the home I had grown up in so much, but going back at the time wasn't an option.

Too afraid to be alone, I entertained abusive relationships that served a buffet of betrayal and heartache. I was too fearful to confront my issues and acknowledge that depression and anxiety were actually things that didn't just affect "those other people." As I mentioned earlier, I numbed my confusion and pain by consuming glass after glass of wine each day. Riddled by guilt for not seeing myself in a way I consciously knew I should – beautiful, intelligent and gifted – I masked the inward contention with outward material possessions. I worked my way up until I could afford a nice apartment in Atlanta's Sandy Springs area. I drove a nice car and found myself hanging around people I knew were no good for me. Together, we spent money we didn't have in the night spots of Buckhead.

When I Couldn't Go On, I Surrendered

BUT GOD. When the weight became too cumbersome to bear, with an internal self-loathing I couldn't explain, I cried out to GOD to help me. After the accident and the painful recovery process, I knew something needed to change, and that something would be activated by my choices. I needed a complete overhaul, a relinquishing of bad habits that would eventually curb my challenge with self-fulfilling prophecies. I asked GOD to take it all away – everything that had kept me from living a joyful and purpose-fueled life as a young woman. I wanted to experience real love, to feel safe again, to feel protected, to feel valuable and to acknowledge the gifts I had.

Since my return to Zimbabwe on January 27, 2007, GOD meticulously stripped away the mess, breaking me, yet restoring me all at the same time. GOD cradled me in His arms and answered every prayer I had said to Him several years before, sometimes in an inebriated state.

By the time this "tumour-on-my-left-ovary-potential-stage-one-cancer" chatter came along, the woman I had been and the woman I had become, could not recognize each other. GOD had given me beauty for ashes, awarding me the precious gift of enjoying my femininity, being a wife to a loving husband and mother to two precious souls. I was (and still am) a friend to many, a sister, a daughter to two awesome parents and so much more. Yet here I was, sitting in the doctor's office gripped by a fear that life, as good as I had come to value it over the past few years, could possibly be cut short if I was diagnosed with cancer.

Bracing for the War Against a New Fear – Disease

The doctor gave me a moment to compose myself before she went on to explain that it was too soon to tell what I was facing. All she could tell me concretely was that I had an 8 cm long tumour growing on my left ovary and that could very well have been the reason why I suffered from an irregular menstrual cycle and extreme fatigue over the preceding weeks. The tumour marker exams she had called for showed conflicting results, so there was need to carry out further tests. She asked me if I needed to call someone. I did. My husband listened on the other side of the phone as I consciously tried to hide the panic in my voice. I was weak, and there he was on the other side of the phone, trying his best to be strong for me and to keep me from having a minute of total breakdown while he was too far away to comfort.

Five minutes later, I left the doctor's office with a prescription in hand. So many thoughts went through my head. I loved life too much to believe what they, the doctors (the whole lot of them I had seen that week), were saying. What about my husband and my children, mom and dad? I am their only daughter! I'm not ready to leave them and the great assignments that lie ahead of me, I kept telling myself. GOD, I love them too much to leave them! Help me!

What Fear Does

It's funny how your mind takes you on a hundred meter dash to the worst possible scenarios at the sound of bad news. I didn't even allow room for the possibility that the results could have been in error or that the tumour was benign. That's what fear does. It wipes away any thoughts opposing it. I looked at the prescription and caught myself asking whether the pills prescribed could magically make what just happened disappear. But they wouldn't. As I watched the pharmacist in the medicine shop downstairs comb through the shelves behind her, I heard my husband's voice behind me. I don't know how fast he must have driven to get to me within minutes, but he had. He gave me hug. In the pharmacy aisle, we just stood in silence, me in his arms, so desperate to tear the pharmacy apart and lash out at someone. But to what end? We didn't know enough. We just had to wait for that dreaded, now third, opinion.

Life's Challenges: A Breeding Ground for Fear or Platform for Profound Faith

My relationship with GOD has taught me lots of things since surviving a suicide attempt, the near fatal car accident, kicking alcoholism, acknowledging and believing that GOD had a plan for my life and journeying through life from depressed state to one in which I let GOD work in me. In my book titled "Reinvented: Challenging Insecurity to Live Authentically Through Faith," I outline many of the difficult experiences I endured and how my faith was forged on account of GOD's providence throughout each ordeal. I also talk about how each of us in life will face seasons of great pain and difficulty that will at times force us to question who we are, the relationships we share and if GOD is even present – or real. These difficult times can and should never be compared with those of another because in our uniqueness, we exhibit even greater differences in the levels to which we accept or deal with strife, pain or struggle.

As I awaited the date of my surgery to approach, I journeyed through time, remembering all the things GOD had cleansed me of. Yes, I was a work in progress, living in a constant state of fighting fear with faith and repenting when I failed at it. **Philippians 1:4-6 New International Version (NIV) states:** *"In all my prayers for all of you, I always pray with joy 5 because of your partnership in the gospel from the first day until now, 6 being confident of this, that he who began a good work in you will carry it on to completion until the day of Christ Jesus.*

I was so desperate to live, and even more desperate to experience the miracles I had heard so many testify of before – that GOD had healed them from disease, that GOD had suddenly done it! I went into mental and spiritual fighting mode, crying out to GOD with all I had within me. GOD listened. A few weeks after the first pronouncement that I had a tumour on my left ovary, I was woken up from post-surgery slumber by the team of surgeons that operated on me. They told me that – get this – the 8 cm tumor was in fact a clump of dead cells that had formed from a burst cyst over time. There was not one cancerous cell in my body! I don't know what happened, but this was the miracle that I had prayed for!

Doing Life Fearlessly is a Choice We Must All Make

Since my recovery, which lasted close to three months (I was awarded a clear diagnosis in March 2017), GOD continues to remind me that He was, still is and will always be on the throne. He has instructed us countless times to have no fear because He is with us. It's time we listened. I share these and other stories of my journey, not from a place of fear, but from a place of knowing that fear and faith cannot coexist. The fight of faith over fear is ongoing; quite literally a full-time job! Life will throw us curve balls that our hearts, minds and bodies may at times fail to comprehend. The enemy is constantly on the prowl, bringing forward distractions designed to derail us from our destiny. BUT GOD.

I can only speak of what I know is true, what I know as fail-proof. GOD has called on us countless times to have no fear, handing us the choice to listen or seek to do life our way. Our way is tiresome. Our way keeps us constantly within reach of the clasps of fear. To get through life, one must carry some belief in a power higher than themselves. I speak of the Highest Power that has transformed my life and saved me time after time after time – from the clasps of depression, the perils of alcoholism that temporarily masked my pain, suicidal thinking, heartbreak, and attacks to my mind, body and spirit.

Receive GOD's Help and Faith Over Fear

No matter what has worn you out or kept you from living the life you envisioned for yourself, choked out your ambition or deterred you from seeing yourself by GOD's design, call out to GOD for help. He heals. He restores. Fear bows down to the sound of GOD's instruction and so does every form of disease. Depression, insecurity, approval addiction and other forms of addiction including alcoholism, abuse, poor self-esteem, diminishing self-worth – I have suffered all of these issues whose foundations carry fear as a key ingredient. 2 Corinthians 1:3-4 states:

"Praise be to the God and Father of our Lord Jesus Christ, the Father of compassion and the God of all comfort, 4 who comforts us in all our troubles, so that we can comfort those in any trouble with the comfort we ourselves receive from God."

I testify in the hope that you too can be convinced to seek the ultimate sources of fearlessness – a living, breathing, committed relationship with GOD, and faith so strong that it motivates you to action even without a guarantee.

I believe one of the best ways to combat fear is to acknowledge the areas in which you struggle with it. Name one of your biggest fears (don't worry, you are not alone).

_____

_____

_____

_____

My journey has taught me that disease is not just limited to a physical attack on your body, but is often times a manifestation of dis-ease or uneasiness, in any other aspect of your life. What areas in your life do you believe are fraught with disease? Outline what you believe will be the ultimate cure.

_____

_____

_____

_____

TRUTH

BY SHANI FARMER

dear fear, you can't have my ...

Dear fear,

    You will no longer paralyze my truth. For so long, you've made me believe I wasn't good enough. You made me believe that my voice was not being heard. You made me believe I wasn't intelligent enough, made me believe it was other people who felt this way about me, when in reality it was all in my own head. I created stories about myself that were untrue. As of today, a dose of God's truth of how beautifully and wonderfully made I am has relinquished what had paralyzed my mind, body and spirit. I rebuke all the negative talk against myself and stand firm in my boldness of truth. What is my truth, you ask? I am loving, fierce, capable beyond all measures, disciplined, and a queen in all areas of my life. I am a wife, an educator. I am empowered and a sister to lean on. I am full in who God has called me to be!

Signed,
Shani

You Can't Have My Truth

I sat there on my plush, white sofa staring out of my floor to ceiling windows overlooking the Alexandria skyline. With my legs folded Indian style and body bent over a fur pillow, I felt my grasp getting tighter and tighter while steadily crying tears of pain. I literally felt like death had invaded my body, slowly paralyzing my limbs. Another chapter of tears from a man that chose to break my heart. Here I was, a woman claiming to be after God's own heart; confident, virtuous and faith driven with values. But the gentle whispers of "I love you" and "I want to be with you forever" that rung in my ear when this man spoke, transitioned my hope of security, longevity and completion into a human being and not God. See, hope for me as a believer is to desire something greater. I expect it, I plan for it and design it.

In my somber moments, I desperately wanted those characteristics to be driven by God's will for my life, but instead I gave that power to a man who had no desire to cover me, protect me and love me. Instead, he played with my love and insulted my loyalty. In return, I gave him my glory by delighting him with my treasures of royalty that most men would only dream of. You see, this had become a cycle for me; stained pillows, puffy eyes and smeared mascara. You know how it is. You're out at a lounge with your girls because you tell yourself there is no way I would meet the right guy at a professional event, or through a friend, or at church. I'm not the girl with that kind of luck. At least that's what I told myself. I didn't quite understand the true meaning of being a child of God, meaning that I already manifest greatness.

My path is already aligned, so I just need to continue to walk in my destiny. God had already established when and where I would meet the man he had for me, I just needed to trust him. Nope! I didn't trust God enough back then, I wanted to be in control. So I masked my tears with mascara, dressed my wounded heart in stilettos and the perfect mini dress, and turned that pain into a fake smile to kill.

The mascara stains did not begin that way. On a chilly Thursday evening while out with my girls, I caught his eye and my heart jumped with excitement! This is it! He's fine, clean as all get up, smells good and has a swag that invigorates every tingle in-between. Could he be the one? I allowed my heart and imagination to run wild with this man because it "felt good." I exposed my vulnerabilities and took on a wife role with no signed contract. I invited myself in and transitioned to the woman I thought he needed. I took over the kitchen to make sure he was fed, engaged in deep conversations, hanging onto every word and inkling of hope he sent me while subconsciously preparing for the next step. I swapped keys with him and moved a few things into his place to show that a rented space had been claimed; all being done without the assurance of any true commitment. I told him my wants and desires while he laid me on my back and entered my sanctuary; the most sacred and worshipped place of a woman's being. Once this happened, he drifted a little. Phone calls went unanswered, hanging with his boys became more prevalent and talks of commitment became "I think we should just let it flow." His flow seemed to always bring me to this furry plush pillow with black mascara stains deeply woven into its center.

What's woven deep into your center? Meaning, what are you focusing on and manifesting into your life? Is it loneliness, brokenness or insecurity? Shattered dreams and unfinished pursuits? The agony of not being married while you watch your friends walk down the aisle? Whatever it is that you have convinced yourself is your truth, I am here, my dear sister, to reassure you that this chapter can be edited. I want to inspire you to walk this journey toward marriage while following God's calling for your life. You have the power to align your center on God and watch him work! And that's exactly what I began to do.

In 2013, after one of the worst breakups of my life, I decided it was time to reinvent the wheel. I started with a physical and emotional detox. I took the time to purge things out of my life. This included toxic people, poisonous emotions and constant negative thoughts. I was very uncomfortable in this new space; having a heavy heart and insecurities were all I knew. Detoxing took me through many levels of emotions. I became sad, angry, confused and downright depressed, but I had hope. I had a desire to begin taking the necessary steps to do things God's way. Not for a moment was I perfect in this walk. I needed constant reminders and accountability on this path. I desired for God to protect me while I was in this season, and that's exactly what he did. Psalm 37:4 says "seek your happiness in the Lord and he will give you your heart's desire." I desired to believe in his promise and I desired to seek God's happiness, not man's.

I wanted to be a wife, so I had to start behaving like one before I became one. And no sis, I do not mean I laid up under some man that was not my husband. I mean I cleansed myself. I cleaned my dirty plate that was filled with scum, scrubbed away all men in my life, rinsed away the hurt that agonized my spirit by taking it to the word of God, and I set my pretty little self right on the shelf until God was ready to reveal me. As I waited patiently on my shelf, I never let the dust settle. I kept the plate fresh by studying the word, surrounding myself with women who were like minded and supportive, and finally allowed God to ignite my ordained glory. My sister, I want you to petition all of your desires to the Lord and be prepared to live in expectations he will summon from within you. You have to know the fullness of you before you can truly identify what it is that you want in someone else. I learned this lesson in my purging of men. I could not see God's vision for my life because my heart and mind were focused on what I needed to do to make these men want me as their wife. A man can sense a woman who is desperate, and they're either going to leach onto your desperation (weakening your ability to be strong and grow into your fullness) or they are going to run from you. God purposely took me through a season of loneliness that forced me to rely solely on him to begin working on the woman he already created me to be. In this season, He gave me the desire to start my own business, whose specific mission would be to empower women to live boldly through a lifestyle of beauty, faith and power. As I was building my business, my business was building me. So today, what desire has God placed on your heart that isn't being fulfilled? Did he tell you to apply for that next position? Did he tell you to be still? Should you be starting that business that will allow you to be stretched? Ask yourself these questions while he purges you and molds you into your destiny. You have to know yourself before committing to a journey of oneness with someone else. As you become one with your partner, you intertwine your souls that possess the good, bad and ugly. Allow for that inter-oneness to begin with your heart and spirit first to become the best version that you can offer to your future spouse.

When my husband Ben and I met, a newfound excitement entered me. Maybe it was his smile or his calm spirit or even his gentleman-like qualities; nevertheless, it grabbed my attention and at the same time raised my guards. As intriguing as this young man was, it was important for me to move differently than I had in the past. I was growing into a woman who knew exactly what she wanted and I was not willing to compromise the best of who I was. I was also keenly aware of what my spirit told me. It struck differently with him and God had prepared me to do things his way. On our second date, with a girlish smile and kind heart, I expressed to Ben that I was in a season of dating with purpose (this translated to dating for marriage). He was a bit perplexed about what I was asking of him. This conversation was intriguing, but completely opposite of what he was used to. Dating with purpose comes with a plan and expectation that is specifically designed with God's purpose at the root of it. Dating with purpose will go against everything that you know to be true. Romans 12:2 tells you not to conform to the pattern of this world, but be transformed by the renewing of your mind. This is a purpose-driven growth moment for you and is vital to the integrity of a sustained marriage. There will be a shift in your mindset, your conversation will change, you will see yourself positioning your relationships with friends to align with your ending goal. Understand that this type of dating will test your ability to be disciplined. Learning how to control your behaviors now will lend a helping hand to the challenges that may arise in your marriage. It was difficult for us to transition into this way of thinking. Questions continuously flowed through our minds creating challenging and compromising moments for us. We would literally stop and ask ourselves, So no sex, no playing house and no spending the night with each other? The answer had to be no, helping me to learn the strength we all possess within. I was letting go of the need to depend on a man and instead depended on my faith to see me through. So my question for you is, what areas of your life do you need to be more disciplined in? Are you ready to renew your mind so that you may walk in your God-given purpose?

Making the decision to date with purpose got me a ring 1 year and 2 months after meeting! I received this ring from a man that was not ready for marriage at all when we met, but with a transitioned mind and following God's plan for our life, I literally jumped out of a plane into the hands of a man who asked me to be his wife.

He Proposed. Now What?

Ben and I learned an important lesson from a close friend of ours during our proposal. He said, "As exciting as this moment is, do not forget to continue to grow individually so that you can be better for one another collectively." We continued to dedicate ourselves during our journey to this purpose. We attended group marriage counseling, we read books that focused on finances, sex in marriage, the psychology of a man and woman, marital expectations and the list goes on. We took our time to design the life we wanted with God's hand always in the midst. I am thankful for the wise counsel and nights of sitting in the car for hours discussing our differences; but just like diamonds, the pressure pressed upon us to live right helped manifest this sacred jewel we can now call marriage.

It was nothing but God's grace, favor, and our faith to follow the direction he had for our lives that allowed us to become each other's overflow. We can stand firmly in our truths and say that it all came through our obedience and staying strong during those times of adversity. Honestly speaking, to say we were perfect would not be the truth, but we never gave up and I can now say the destination reached was well worth the journey taken. So when I walked down the aisle in my hot pink diamond stilettos, fitted gown that enhanced and danced on every curve, I walked with a new found confidence. I gave my desires to God, set a standard of expectation, planned for what I wanted and patiently prepared myself to receive this life I dreamed of when I sat on that couch holding that plush pillow stained with my dark mascara.

I challenge you, my sister, to try something different. To put your fears aside and hope for what you want by desiring marriage from God's standards, expecting him to fulfill his promise, planning to be the best you for your future mate and designing a life that goes beyond what you could dream.

What are your fears of dating God's way?

_____

_____

_____

_____

How do you plan to overcome these fears?

_____

_____

_____

_____

PROMISE

BY CHINITA IRBY

dear fear, you can't have my ...

Dear fear,

You are exposed! It is time everyone knew the real truth about you. Fear, you are False Evidence Appearing Real. No longer will you control my thoughts and decisions. The relationship we had is over! I am walking away and never looking back. I am pressing toward the promises that are ahead. My father assures me that faith shows the reality of what I hope for; it is the evidence of things I cannot see. So, you can't have what God has promised me. He promised me an abundant life, a life filled with peace, joy, healing and restoration. You whispered to me for the final time. I declare, I am who God says I am. I am fearfully and wonderfully made in His image. I have dominion and authority over you! My faith in God and His promises is increasing, and you are decreasing. You can't have my promises!

Signed,
Chinita Irby
Unshakable Faith

You Can't Have My Promise of Healing and Restoration

◆————————————————————◆

"Don't be afraid, for I am with you. Don't be discouraged, for I am your God. I will strengthen you and help you. I will hold you up with my victorious right hand." Isaiah 41:10 NLT

I attempted to share my story many times prior to now, but was paralyzed by this four letter word fear. What would people think if they knew the truth? The story of my life and what happened the summer of 1984 attempted to steal my promises. But I decided, NO. God decided it was time to share my story and receive total healing and restoration from what tried to break me. It is my sincere prayer that what once had me bound will no longer be a stronghold in your life after reading this chapter. The captives have been set free!

Thank God I don't look like what I've been through! Being the oldest of three siblings carries a great deal of responsibility and comes with high expectations. I grew up in a small rural town in Dallas County, Alabama known as Beloit, Alabama. Unlike most children, I don't remember most of my early childhood. I began to suppress memories of my childhood at a young age. I guess that is sometimes true for children growing up in abusive homes. You see, I grew up in a home with a father and mother, but the home was anything but peaceful. I remember hearing my mother screaming for help and pleading with my father to not hit her. This was a constant, day after day.

It was during this time that I believe FEAR crept in. From day to day, I never knew the mood of my father. My mother and I walked on eggshells and hoped that we would not say or do anything to upset him. I didn't want him to hit her and I didn't want to hear her cry. It was at this time that fear taught me if I conform to what a person does or says, all will be well with me, even if I don't agree with what is said or done. At least, that is what I use to think and believe. The constant mental and physical abuse my mother suffered at the hands of my father led up to a day I will never forget.

It was the summer of 1984, and my father arrived home from work. He was unusually quiet. My mother, four year old sister, and two year old brother were in the kitchen. My mother was preparing dinner and my sister and brother were sitting in the middle of the kitchen floor playing. I was in the room that doubled as a bedroom and living room watching television. The quiet didn't last long. I heard my mother and father begin to argue and my mother decided she was going to take us and leave him that day. That day was just one of many days she decided to leave, but she would always return. As an adult, I often asked her what kept her coming back and she could never answer me. This day, she got us and got into the car to leave, but was stopped by my father with a rifle. My father decided that we were not leaving him that day. I remember him sitting in the middle of our driveway with a loaded rifle ready to shoot into the car if we tried to leave. I was terrified and filled with fear at the thought of him shooting into the car. I had seen many sides of my father, but never to this extent. He was angry; maybe angry is an understatement. I attempted to tell my mom how we could

84

escape and leave without going out the main driveway. She got us out of the car and we went back into the house. My father followed us back into the house and was really angry that she had attempted to leave. I sat on the sofa crying and wondering how we would get out of our home without being killed. Yes, killed. My father often said I was just like my mom. I wondered what he meant by that statement, but there is no doubt in my mind that he would have killed the family and perhaps himself that night. We got in the car for a second time in an attempt to escape. We were not successful. He sat in the middle of the driveway with his rifle each time. I believe we attempted at least three times to leave. Each time, we went back into the house, him pursuing us with his rifle. Each time, upon entering the house I sat on the sofa. This time was no different, except my favorite show was on television, Duck Man. I really enjoyed watching this show. I was sitting on the sofa watching the show and thinking about how we could escape. I heard one single gunshot. I ran into the next room and saw my father sitting in the chair next to the kitchen door. I knew he was dead when I walked into the room. He did not move or say anything as I walked past the chair he was slouched in. My brother and sister were in the kitchen sitting in the middle of the floor and my mother was in the kitchen hysterical. Remember when I said that being the oldest carries a great deal of responsibility and high expectations? It was my responsibility to get my mother, sister and brother out of our home and to our neighbor's home. I realized as we were leaving, that my mother was acting very strange. I later learned that she had experienced a nervous breakdown. She had to stay in the hospital for a while after this traumatic ordeal. I was only ten years old at the time, but I had suddenly become the caretaker for my mother, sister, and younger brother. I experienced what no child should have to experience at any age.

I know the experiences in my childhood shaped who I became as a young woman. As I matured in age and began dating, often I chose men like my father. My father was physically in our home, but he was emotionally unavailable. This was my norm as a child, and it followed me into adulthood. Can you identify with being with someone physically, but emotionally he or she is inaccessible? Often we imitate what we have been exposed to in our childhood, and the vicious cycle continues. I was looking for love in all the wrong places and in all the wrong men. The behavior of my father was the only representation of what I thought was love. But, let me tell you about another man I met who is love. Jesus is love! He loves you and me so much that he knows the number of hairs on our head (Matthew 10:30 NLT). Now that is love!

I didn't recognize this pattern at the time, but as time passed and I allowed God to heal and restore me, He showed me the basis of my decisions. A turning point for me was at the age of thirty-seven, being pregnant for the first time. I was single and alone. It is during times like this that fear comes in, and it always brings company. Fear brought rejection. I was fearful of being in a relationship. I did not want to be rejected, just as my father had rejected my mother and his family. I quickly realized it was no longer about me, it was all about my unborn son. My son is my greatest accomplishment! My son gives me the courage to love. I hug him and tell him I love him often. I demonstrate love at all times, even when I discipline. I teach him to always show the love of Christ.

I live my life in the present and not in the past. I love with purpose and on purpose. I am intentional with my love. I have non-negotiables and deal breakers. A specific deal breaker is not being able to communicate openly. What are your non-negotiables and deal breakers? My prayer is that the Lord continues to makes me BETTER and not BITTER. Am I totally healed and restored? No, but I am on my way to total healing and restoration. Does fear attempt to rear its ugly head? Yes, every now and then. I release the word of God over my situation and fear has to bow down and flee. Fear is defeated and cut down at the root. I committed five years ago, after the birth of my son, to allow God to do the work in my life; heal and restore me. It is His desire that you and I are free in every area of our life. I challenge you to deny all thoughts of fear and rejection. Dear Fear, you can't have our promises of healing and restoration! The captives are set free!

How has fear robbed you of your healing and restoration?

_____

_____

_____

What steps will you take today toward total healing and restoration?

_____

_____

SLINGSHOT
BY CHRISTINE HANDY

dear fear, you can't have any ...

Dear fear,

Yes, you have been in my head. I kick myself for even allowing you space there. Yes, I walk around confident. And yes, I have experienced success. I have overcome so many hurdles, despite you. From the time I stepped onto the campus of Old Dominion University to start my freshman year to graduating from George Washington University with my doctorate degree, you have tried to deter me and stop me from reaching my goals. But to God be the glory! Oh yes, I graduated from ODU, and I finished my doctorate degree after ten long years of interrupted study, despite you. I won a major election to serve as the President of a prestigious national organization, despite you. When you get in my head, you try to tell me what I can't do, what I shouldn't pursue, and what hurdles or roadblocks will come my way. BUT, I thank God that my faith prevails. When you jump into my head with your ugly voice, I have learned to be like a computer and use my pop-up blocker. It's your negative talk, not mine. Better than a pop-up blockers, is the delete button. Poof, you are gone! I replace your ugly words with encouraging words, with positivity. You can't have space here!

From now on, I will not allow you to talk to me. I will talk to myself! No, I am not crazy. I am attacking the Giant – YOU! I remind myself daily of David and that Giant Goliath and know that David was victorious. So Dear Fear, you can't have my slingshot! You are going down! I'm taking control of my mind and my life today. Victory shall be mine. David was victorious, and so am I! Now that's how you talk to yourself! I AM a winner!

Yours Truly,
Dr. Christine Handy

You Can't Have My Slingshot

I was scared straight when we pulled up to that dorm.
My guardian angel, a lady who looked out for me when I was
homeless, dropped me off at Gresham Hall at Old Dominion
University and wished me luck. I didn't tell her, but I didn't want
her to leave me. I wanted her to go in with me and pretend she
was my mom. When she hugged me to say good bye, I wanted
to hold on and not let go. BUT, I had to be brave, I had to be
a tough chick! The fraternity boys were everywhere, walking
up and down the stairs, going from car to car, helping all the
newbies to unload and transform empty dorm rooms into homey
bedrooms and places to study. Two frat guys walked up and
looked at me strangely. I didn't understand why they seemed
puzzled. One said, "Is that all you got?" They both looked at my
green trunk that I had proudly purchased from Walmart. "Yes,
this is it", I responded. They looked at each other and then at
me, shrugged their shoulders, and then helped me take my one
and only item upstairs to the third floor. Everything I had was in
that trunk - my comforter, my clothes, my school supplies, my
toiletries, and my alarm clock. Yep, that was all I had, and it was
all in that trunk. I didn't even know what I didn't have, after all,
I was homeless, having spent the last six months sleeping on my
guardian angel's daughter's bedroom floor. All I knew, was I was
realizing my dream, I was going to college.

You see college was my ticket out of poverty, it was my ticket to a
better life, it was my ticket to all that I had dreamed about. The
dorm was busy, everyone was moving back and forth, others had

their families helping them to set up their room, parents were meeting other parents and students were meeting other students, but all I had was me, and this ugly voice in my head. "Who do you think you are, you can't go to college? You won't fit in here, look at you, you have all your stuff in one little trunk, you're just a poor little black girl, how many people do you see that look like you, what are you doing at this school, they're going to eat you alive, you don't even have stuff, look at you, who do you think you are showing up here?" I talked back, "The devil is a liar, I am going to make it here, I will get a degree, I will survive this, me and my trunk!"

AND then I met my roommate. She too thought it was strange that all I had was that trunk. She was also surprised that her roommate was Black. I'm just keeping it real. The tension was thick. We were totally different, I got up early, she got up late, I stayed up late, she went to bed early, I liked R&B music, she liked Country music, she washed her hair every day and I didn't (she thought that was gross, lol) and I could list more. That ugly voice showed up: "She hates you, she doesn't want you for a roommate, why are you here, you don't belong here, you can't afford this." I was trying hard not to listen to that voice. I heard my grandmother's sweet voice, the one who always encouraged me and told me I could do whatever I put my mind too, the one who quoted scripture to me, "You can do all things through Christ who strengthens you", "In this world you will have trials and tribulations, but fear not", I'll stop right there. The word says, "Fear not." It wasn't the first time that I had to put a stop to that ugly voice and replace it with positive thoughts. I remembered the voice of Ms. Horne, my favorite English teacher at Hampton

High School, she told me, "You are a smart girl, you can go to college, don't worry about the finances, it will work itself out, you just get there." I was holding on to that thought. It was then that I learned the power of positive thinking, the power of replacing negative thoughts with positive thoughts, the power of encouraging yourself. (By the way, in less than four weeks, my roommate moved out of the dorm, I never knew why.)

Why was I at ODU? It was a few reasons. It wasn't far from my hometown, Hampton, Virginia, they gave me a few scholarships designated for minorities, and ok, I will admit it, my boyfriend was going there too. He played basketball in high school and had lots of offers. He chose ODU and was there on a full scholarship. I was excited about this next chapter in my life. He was from Norfolk, Virginia and we had a distance friendship, having lived 45 minutes apart. We were now going to the same college. On the first day of classes, I went to a long and boring science class and was shocked to be in a lecture hall with more than 150 students in the class (or at least that is what it seemed like in my 50+ year old memory). After class I went to visit my boyfriend, who didn't live in a dorm. Since he was on the basketball team, he lived in campus apartments. One of his roommates let me in and that was when I made an astounding discovery. Sitting in the living room was another girl who was also a student at ODU and I immediately recognized her. She went to his high school, a cheerleader that I saw when I went to a few basketball games there and when I went to his prom. Not sure what was happening, I discovered that he had purposefully locked himself in his bedroom when he heard my voice. Why? Because he had two girlfriends and we were both in his living room. We were all at the same college. What was he thinking? A coward, he locked himself in his bedroom and wouldn't come out. I exchanged a few words with her to figure out what the deal was and I headed to the front door. On my way out, I let her know that she could have him. I wanted no parts of these shenanigans. My ugly voice showed up – "Ha ha, what a fool, you don't belong here, the joke is on you, you thought he loved you, he played you big time!" What a way to start college, the first day of class. I wanted to cry, I wanted to scream, I was heartbroken, but I had to be strong, I had to be a tough chick! AND I had to talk back to that ugly voice. "I deserve better! Thank you, Lord, for that revelation on the first day of class, perfect timing!"

I struggled through the year financially, it was tough. I worked on campus in the Language Lab on Work Study and made a little spending money. I remember one of my younger siblings sending me $5 in an envelope. Knowing I was struggling, he wanted to be helpful. My little sister did the same thing. Oh, how I loved them! They wanted to help their older sister and it was the sweetest thing. This memory brings tears to my eyes today. It was tough being on my own with no financial assistance from anywhere. Sometimes when others that lived on the same dorm floor as I did ordered pizza, they asked, "who wants in". I wanted in, but I could not afford to donate $5 to pizza slices as most of the time that was all I had. The ugly voice- "lol, you can't even buy pizza, what are you doing here?" I hated that ugly voice, "Stop talking to me!"

At Thanksgiving, I visited my grandmother. She wanted to know how everything was going. I said, "Grandma, I don't feel like I belong there, I don't have money like the other students,

I couldn't even buy all my books, I don't have clothes like the other girls, I don't even have a pillow." She looked at me and said, "Don't ever let me hear you talk like that! You are a child of the King! Trouble don't last always my dear, weeping may endure for a night, but joy comes in the morning! You keep going to that school, stop talking negative, you are a smart girl and I know you can do it, you are going to graduate from that college and go on to do great things in your life. You are a special granddaughter and grandpa and I, we don't have much, but we will help you when we can"....... and then she took me to the store and bought me a pillow.

So that is how my college education journey started. I did well academically at ODU, I had a sweetheart, eventually moved off campus and life seemed good, but I continued to struggle through school financially and many times heard that ugly voice. "Who do you think you are? You can't go to that dance, it's too dressy. You can't spend money on that, you can barely buy groceries." Sometimes the voice was right, and I just made excuses to my friends as to why I wasn't going, sometimes I reached out to one of my sweet Sorority sisters and borrowed a dress, and consistently, I talked back to that ugly voice. "You will not make me feel bad about this, I am going to be okay, it's not that important, it won't always be this way." And my favorite line was, "One day!" After all, that is why I was going to school. Old Dominion University was an amazing experience for me. I connected with lifelong friends, got involved in school activities, was a leader on campus, pledged Delta Sigma Theta Sorority, Inc., and met the most astounding, smart, and successful young women, whom I am forever connected to. I earned my

Bachelor of Science Degree in Special Education and went on to graduate school from there. Today, I am a successful high school principal, have a Doctorate Degree in Education Leadership and Public Policy and am the president of a prestigious national organization.

I   learned a lot from my challenges, lessons that continue to impact me today. I learned to never give up, be persistent, push forward, write the vision and make it plain, hard work pays off, be a leader, stay focused on my goals, pray, have faith, cherish mentors and friendships, and never to be a victim of my circumstances. My biggest lesson though, is about that voice. That ugly voice does exist and hearing it doesn't mean that you are crazy unless you choose to listen to it. I refused to listen to this negative talk in my head. Like a computer, I put up pop up blockers and most times, just hit the delete button. I replaced it with positive thinking and positive affirmations. Basically, I spoke positivity over my life and refused to let negativity guide me. One of my favorite stories in the bible is about David and the giant Goliath. When David faced that Giant, he believed that he would win. He put on the full armor of God and slayed that Giant with his faith and a slingshot. So, whenever I face a giant, I activate my faith and tell myself, "Always remember that David was victorious!" and like David, I take my slingshot, and I always win.

Questions for you:

Have you lost your mind? You better! When you change your mind, you change your life. What does "fear" sound like in your head?

_____

_____

_____

Now write some positive self-talk to replace that negative talk. Ex. I can do this, I will win. I Am a winner!

_____

_____

_____

RESET

BY B. JACQUELINE JETER

dear fear, you can't take my ...

Dear fear,

I know you are listening and watching. We've been together so long, I can't even remember when we first met. Was it when the kids pretended to be my friend, only to reveal the set up by encircling me and taunting me until I ran home crying? Was it when I got my first car and the insta-friends I acquired only used me to get places and then abandoned me once there? Honestly, I saw the signs early, like one does with any toxic relationship, but I thought maybe it would change or maybe I can handle this on my own. As time went on, I realized you were set in your ways with no desire to change. Your main mission was not to bring anything good to my life, but to keep me cowering in bondage and a negative self-image. I use the word dear in the highest sarcastic tone possible because there is nothing 'dear' about this abusive relationship.

You have kept me isolated from family, friends, opportunities, and most importantly the passion and purpose for my life. In some odd way, I gained strength from you. I was secure in knowing that if no one else was there, you would certainly be there, whispering to me that no matter what I accomplished there was someone better. Well, the once whimpering baby girl, protected and sheltered by her family and her imaginary world has wiped her nose and dried her eyes.

Allow me to introduce myself. My name is Barbara Jacqueline Jeter. I will no longer allow you to take anything else from me. I am taking back everything you held hostage; time, self-esteem, wisdom and opportunities. This revolution or RESET will be televised, as I want the whole world to see your defeat! You will not recover from this blow. Please accept this note as your eviction notice. When you try to attend, you will find all locks changed and points of entry blocked and sealed. Fear, you thought you would stop me with whispers of being too old or that it was too late. Guess what—you lose. I've only just begun to be awesome! YOU CANNOT HAVE MY RESET!

Sincerely,
Jacqueline Jeter

You Can't Have My Reset

◆————————————————————◆

Reset (verb) re·set \ (.)rē- set \ : 1: to set again or anew 2: to change the reading of often to zero

I remember the moment like it just happened. It was a sunny Friday in October when I received that congratulatory phone call welcoming me to the pharmaceutical world at one of the world's premier pharma companies. Everyone in my area wanted to work there. No more two jobs. I had now arrived at a pivotal point in my life and career. I knew it was my time because I always got a feeling of unrest in my spirit when I was about to move on. The move proved to be an easy transition from the pharmacy to corporate America, and the beginning of an awesome adventure of discovery.

From the glorious moment of my earth entry until now, God has consistently showered me with favor. This opportunity was no different. While favor was there, the other 'f' word, fear, was also lurking. When I went to science camp at 9, instead of the required age of 12, fear was there. When I was the only 'me' in most of my classes from elementary to high school, fear was there. Like a shadow, you cloaked me all my life. Fear, your picture should be in the post office as a most wanted stalker. You have no shame. If it wasn't for the support of my awesome parents and oldest sister, I could have easily buckled to the fear of not being good enough and second guessing myself. I could have stayed bound by possible rejection when I entered oratorical contests, made straight As, or when I ran and won student government offices in high school and college. I could blame all of it on fear, but truth is I never pushed you away. I didn't scream or seek help. You became my addiction at one point. My life didn't seem normal if you were not there looking over my shoulder at every move.

Like clockwork, there you were as I walked into the lab the first day of my new, coveted job. You were there when I met my newly hired younger colleagues, whispering your familiar unsweet nothings that made me question if making this move was too late in my life. After all, I was 27 and they were fresh out of college. As I became more comfortable in the intellect with which God had blessed me, I gained a confidence that seemed to find your mute button. You left me alone for a while, at least up until the time I moved into a new, more demanding role. There you were, waiting in my new office next to the flowers from my friends. I could see that you too had gained confidence because your whispers became louder and more frequent, but your message was the same—you are too old for this new position. You almost made me miss the opportunity of a lifetime to travel to a week-long global training conference in London with your whispers of fear. Fear that I would get lost, or that my colleagues wouldn't like me because I was new. The more my passport stamps grew, the more you came with your intimidation game trying to keep me grounded; however, I found strength in the Lord to keep me focused. You became so desperate to paralyze me that you almost talked me out of receiving a promotion, saying that it would take up all my time and that I would not have time for anything or anyone else. It was just another of your lies.

You really went off the rails when I became a manager of others, not only by causing me to question my leadership ability, but also to interject fear into my direct reports to the point that they thought I was trying to hurt their careers. Thankfully, God cleared that up in a fashion that could only be done by Him. Just as quickly as you reappeared, you faded to black again after that. Years passed, until the time there was a departmental headcount reduction exercise where we had to reapply for our jobs. Your whispers took on a different tone this time. I remember you asking me, why would such a powerful company want to keep some dime-a-dozen woman from small town western NC? What makes you think that you are true competition to people with Masters and doctorate degrees? I cried that night and didn't sleep due to the anxiety brought on by your whispers. It took God to remind me that He had kept me already through two mergers and one previous headcount reduction. Your script stayed the same several years later during the next headcount reduction, but I reminded myself this time of God's keeping power.

Fast forward to right before my 22nd anniversary with this same company. I began to get that same restless feeling that came over me whenever God moved me from department to department. I pursued opportunities within for which I was qualified, but to my surprise, my reward was not a welcome to the team, but a 'thank you for your interest but.' Fear, you resurfaced and wow had you eaten your Wheaties™. I was paralyzed and confused. What was happening? Was I really too old now? Would anyone else hire me if the rumors were true? I mean, I didn't see anyone my age being hired in other areas of the company. I reached out to God for clarity, but He became silent. And like a wailing siren, fear, you became even louder.

Then, one day as I came into work, the rumors started that our company was closing. I knew that was preposterous, but they swirled even the more. Fear graduated from whispers to decibel breaking shouts. Much to my relief, God soon became audible again, and with the following powerful affirmations: **You're safe. It's already taken care of. I've got you covered.** I was immediately saturated with peace beyond understanding. The rumors kept swirling, but my peace kept expanding. During this time of uncertainty, I learned about me. In John Maxwell's book, *The 15 Invaluable Laws of Growth*, he says that in order to grow yourself, you must know yourself. I know that I am enough and a force with which to be reckoned. I know I am a uniquely designed solution for someone's problem.

It was during this time of being pushed out of my comfort zone of a secure, lucrative job that my journey of self-discovery began. I was now facing a future where I didn't know what I was going to do. I made the brief mistake of looking at others and their credentials and accomplishments instead of my own. I was quickly reminded of a quote that the Lord gave me, "Comparison is a thief of purpose." I started to write down every skill set gained and every accomplishment I had achieved over the last 20 plus years. I had been successful and impactful in more ways than I had previously acknowledged, specifically completing a grueling training as a job plus coach. It was in these moments that God revitalized my coaching skills. I found myself supporting my coworkers with their next step life plans. In doing so, I was unofficially developing and writing my own. My black girl magic swagger returned, and the cataracts attached to the vision of my life dried up.

It felt like I had been holding my breath, but was now able just to breathe. Life does indeed begin at 50.

Fear, I still throw my head back in laughter as I think of the look on your face as those three affirmations took the wind right out of your mouth. Peace, focus, confidence and resiliency was reset in my life. I laugh even harder when you, fear, my constant companion, realized that you had been replaced. Please understand it was me, not you. It was me realizing that MY name was on my birth certificate, not yours, therefore taking my life back. It was me feeling your presence but not acknowledging or giving any credence to it. I'm no longer stalling, but allowing your whispers, shouts, and smoke screens to be my launching pads. It was me reclaiming my time, way before Maxine Waters even made it famous, by pursuing my Masters again. It was me enrolling in and becoming an independent certified John Maxwell speaker, teacher and coach as well as starting my own coaching and leadership company, The RippleEffect Coaching and Leadership Group. It was me that started her own encouragement ministry, ReignDrops; seeing triumph in everything. It was me who had the opportunity to pick from 10 new job offers in pharmaceutical development. Fear, God didn't make an empty vessel. I am brilliant and an invaluable asset to any corporation, especially my own.

You see fear, you took what was a beautiful, pristine canvas of my life and colored it with dark blotches, missed opportunities and choked out dreams. However, now the brush is in my hand and I am recoloring every dark spot and stain that you left behind. Yes behind, because that is where you are in my life. You see, I have decided just as definition says, to reset, or set again or anew. In this next phase of my life, I now understand what someone said to me. When you hit 50, life is just beginning. So thank you fear, for helping me realize just how much more life I have to live and what my purpose truly is going forward. Oddly, you coached me right into success. Thanks for the push. When you thought you were holding me down, you were catapulting me forward. My reliance on you caused my rejection, but now I see it was really preparation for the next phase of my life. In case you forgot, age ain't nothing but a number. It's only too late when I am dead. Since I still have a pulse, I have so much more left to do. So fear, this is the last conversation we will be having because this comradery, this communication is over. Your call has been dropped and number blocked. Remember this. I used to look over my shoulder thinking you'd be there; now it is your turn. You see fear, I no longer fear you. My vision has been reset and now it is time for you to fear me.

What dream or desire have you placed on the back burner, thinking that it is too late to pursue?

_____

_____

_____

Are you looking at a rejection as the end or seeing it as catalyst to a new beginning?

_____

_____

_____

DREAMS

BY KIM BROWN

dear fear, you can't have my ...

Dear fear,

I remember my mom telling me that she was trying to live to see her grandson graduate from high school. I looked at her strange, wondering if she was trying to tell me something. My son and I lived all the way on the east coast and she lived in the midwest. We usually came home once a month or every other month. Mom was just fine, and trips back home were almost a vacation for me. I thought that my mommy would always be there for me. She got worse each time I went home. One particular time when I went to the doctor with her, we discussed hospice. I knew right then to never let them take her away from home unless she wanted to go. I made a promise to be there for her as much as possible. Each trip home brought me closer to the reality that I may lose her.

As my mom grew weaker, I just told her to stay. I wasn't ready for her to leave me. She was my foundation and she provided so much wisdom. When she finally left to check out our next location, I hit rock bottom. Fear of the unknown is a beast. It held me so tight, I couldn't breathe. When I lifted my arms, my fear would twist them behind my back. Fear hit me in my knees until I could no longer walk. My lips moved, but no one heard what I had to say. I would gasp for air as if someone was choking me.

While my mom's health was slowly declining, she would continually tell me to pray. God answered my prayers. Slowly, I got back on my feet and I began to take small steps. I knew that I was strong, but I needed her so badly right now because so many things were going wrong. Each time I called with a different issue, she would tell me to pray about it. I prayed so hard for her to stay with me because she was helping me to solve my life problems. What I didn't know was that she was telling me to pray to God for answers to my problems. I'm learning how to walk again, but with a new light. My foundation is being rebuilt, but with more of God and less of me. I know that if God can do it for me, he can do it for you. In church, they would sing that God is an on-time God, and I firmly believe that to be true. The preacher would say that God is a doctor when you need a doctor. He is a lawyer when you need a lawyer. He is a way maker when you don't have a way. I'm here to tell you that he has done all of the above for me and he can do it for you.

God gave me the strength to begin to understand my "next" journey while here on earth. He has closed and is still closing doors that I never thought would be closed. At the same time, he is opening doors that I never thought would be opened. I'm grateful for this journey because I can see that I'm already on the path to being stronger than I was before because I'm stepping out on faith. Often, this journey doesn't make sense, but I just keep taking steps. I keep taking steps as I walk into whatever God has in store for me; walking towards my next with a smile, a little anxiety and fear and with purpose. I'm walking into my next with a purpose and with a foundation that is newly built.

Dear Fear, step aside. You can't have what God has already defined for me. You can't have my NEXT!

Kimberley A. Brown

You Can't Have My Dreams

Ok, I said it. I broke down. I finally broke down. As I walked through the door to the doctor's office, all I could think was to put one foot in front of the other. The nurse called me in, and I greeted her as if nothing was wrong. I couldn't wait to see someone so I could get back to normal. I kept telling them that I couldn't stay focused. I couldn't remember why I walked from one room to another. I forgot to breathe and then I would gasp for air. At night, I would watch the ceiling fan until day break. Have you ever been tired just from living through life's circumstances? I was tired, so I went to bed. I knew I would be safe if I didn't get out of bed. If I just laid there, I didn't have to remember where I was going, what I was going through, nor what I was going after. Mom was the one that I talked to when the world became overwhelming. She knew everything about my career, raising my son and working to keep the bond with his father. My mom knew all of my secrets. Do you know what it's like to lose the one that holds your foundation together? Have you thought about having to tell your support system that it's ok for them to die so they won't feel pain any longer? What would you do if they asked you to give them the dose of morphine that would take out the last little effort, the last functionality of their kidney. I put the dropper in the bottle and sucked up the dosage. I thought for a few minutes about what I was doing, and put a couple drops back in the bottle. I needed her a little longer. Mom settled down and went to sleep, but it didn't last very long.

As my mom grew weaker, I just told her to stay. I wasn't ready for her to leave me. I wrapped my arms around her and whispered it again, "Don't leave me. I'm scared to navigate through this life without you, and I'm tired. I'm tired of fighting and I'm sinking." She told me to go on and get my stuff together. I talked to my mommy about a new career. I put diesel gas in a car that didn't take diesel gas and ended up stranded on the interstate. My pipe burst in the master bath while I was at a conference, ruining the kitchen that I had just remodeled. My son was starting his junior year at college and getting an apartment for the first time. I promised to purchase furniture and decorate for him, but I couldn't get it done. My hair was falling out while my feet were swollen and I was gaining weight from snacking. I didn't even recognize myself when I looked in the mirror. The lines across my forehead were deep and I could see the dark circles that had developed underneath my eyes.

I loved my job. I had been with the same company for 30 years. I started in an entry level position and I was now an officer of the company. My family was so proud of me. My job helped me to be able to pay for some of my mother's expenses. It allowed me to fly her only grandson to see her from college and to pay his college expenses. It provided me with the opportunity to travel back to see about her. The career that I loved so much was coming to an end at the same time that my mommy was dying. The loyalty that I felt to this company and the many years that I had served, regardless of my circumstances, was going to end. Mom had coached me through so many different situations, and she was almost always right about what would happen. She was so worried that I would lose my job and I just kept telling her that we were going to be alright. I didn't want her to worry, but I couldn't hide the stress in my voice about the job. She knew me too well.

My mommy sat up in her chair and told me to go on home and get things together. She said that she would be around for a little bit longer. Instead of a few weeks, my mom gave me another 3 months. As each day slipped by, my heart beat faster. She tried to go to the emergency room, but I went with her and got a room right next to her. My blood pressure had skyrocketed and I fainted. My trips to the doctor were endless. The crack in my foundation was growing wider.

My mom called me by my full name, Kimberley Ann Brown. I came running because I knew something was wrong. She told me that she knew what I had done with the morphine and she needed the full dosage. My hands shook as I sucked up the full dosage in the dropper. I cried all the way back to the family room where I administered one of the final doses of the painkiller that would take my mommy away from me forever. So, I put my big girl panties on and marched. As I faded, to protect myself from the pain and the fear of living without my mommy, my big girl panties turned into hipsters, bikinis and then a thong. I was naked and afraid, and it was visible to everyone that I encountered, or so I thought.

I inhaled so deeply that I honestly didn't know if I would ever be able to catch my breath. What would I do without her? Who would I talk to about everything that was going on in my life? When I got tired, I would go home to mom's house to get my mojo back. The mojo was the magic that happens when I walk through the door. It's the way she has always hugged me since I was a little girl. It's the aroma of the house and the way I breathe in when I give her a hug. She would take a look at me and tell me to just go on upstairs and lay down. For a brief moment in time, I could just stop. I didn't have to be mom because she took over with my son. I didn't have to be the corporate executive, community service worker, nor did I have to curl my hair, wear heels or put on matching clothes. All I had to do was just exhale and relax. This time was different. This time, there wasn't any of the good home cooked meals. She needed help back to her chair in the family room. This time, she asked if I wouldn't mind staying downstairs with her because she wasn't feeling well. I noticed that she was frail, weak and barely holding on. As the tears slowly trickled down my face, I made her a pancake with a little syrup and gave her a glass of soda. She ate half of the pancake, took a few sips of soda and asked me to cover her up because she was cold. Then she looked at me and told me not to be afraid. She said that her time was near, and she closed her eyes and fell asleep.

I peeked around the corner at the funeral home, and a lady was laying in a casket. The funeral home director pointed to the casket and said, "There's your mom." That's not my mom. She ain't in no casket. She's supposed to be at home waiting for me. It was different this time. She just laid there and didn't say anything. She wouldn't get up. I was scared, tired and I just wanted to go with her. Somehow, I made it seem as if everything was ok, but it wasn't. It felt as if it was just too much to handle, so I started to fade because of the pain. I honestly thought that I could talk at the funeral long enough for my mommy to never go away. The fear had finally consumed me. The fear of living without my mommy was overwhelming, but no one knew. I told everyone that I was fine. I went back to work as if nothing was wrong. I attended a conference shortly after the funeral, and it was as if I was back to "normal." When I stepped outside the doors of my house, no one knew my secret. I started working out so I could get back to normal. I wore my effortless makeup that I like so much. My house was clean, the grass was cut and my son was happy and healthy. When I stepped outside my house, it was a picture of perfection. On the outside, I have the perfect career and the perfect family. No one knows my secret. I've learned to manage in fear. At times, I even believe I'm winning.

My reality is that I'm crippled. Fear had me wrapped in a blanket like a newborn. This time, I went home and there was no one there. She didn't answer the door. When I went in, she wasn't in her chair. There wasn't anything cooking on the stove. The phone kept ringing and no one was there to answer. As I closed my eyes, my greatest fears came true. Fear stole my joy. Fear held me until I couldn't breathe. Fear would squeeze me a little tighter each time I tried to get away. My eyes watered like a running faucet. Fear made me believe that joy would never come again. When I couldn't go any further, my fears stood and watched me suffer. If fear would just hit me, it would be so much better. Then they would listen to me because I would have proof.

I heard mom's voice tell me, "Baby, it's going to be alright." She said that my power was in my thoughts, actions, reactions and peace of mind. She told me that she wasn't going anywhere, but she did. My mommy left me when I needed her the most. Have you ever had someone break their promise to you? Have you been abandoned and left alone? She peacefully left me at the hospital. I thought she was asleep, so I stepped into the hallway to make a phone call. The nurse came out to tell me that she was gone. I didn't get to say goodbye. As they led me to the waiting room, I screamed inside, but a low moan came out. She was suppose to come home with me. I told her I was going to take care of her. No one heard me because I was fading, and I was almost gone.

My son and I reversed our roles. He was trying to take care of me, and the sad part was that I was allowing him to do just that. I was actually listening to him. He was following me around so he could pick up my purse, wallet, fans, shirts, brushes, shoes and anything else I would set down and then not remember where they were. He reminded me to take my medicine. He did everything from a distance. He watched me and made sure I was ok. When I began to fall apart, he would swoop in and handle the situation, but I insisted that he return to school. I wasn't crazy. I was just falling apart. And if I fell apart, I needed him to have an education so he could take care of me. That's what I told him. When he left for school and everyone went home, it was quiet.

I got up, mom. I got up. I remembered what you told me and I'm moving forward. You said you would always be there with me, and you were right. I prayed for peace and it happened. It took so long because I miss you so much. I heard myself laugh one day and it startled me. I couldn't remember the last time that I had laughed. My smile returned and I caught myself singing all the wrong words to a song. I took one small step each day, and I started to move forward. God is the source of my strength, and the more I prayed to him, the better my situation became. He sat me down so I could rebuild my foundation. I'm grateful for the trials and tribulations because he has made me stronger than before. Just like you taught me, I'm moving forward fulfilling my dreams and handling my business. Most importantly, I'm building a greater relationship with God. The fear that I had almost got the best of me. It almost crippled my steps and cancelled my dreams, but that's not going to happen. I can't wait to show you my next.

I'm back!

Has someone that meant a lot to you ever broken their promise? How did that make you feel? What did you do?

_____

_____

_____

If you have ever been down and out, how did you firm your foundation so you could step into the next endeavor that God has for you?

_____

_____

_____

IMPACT

BY EDITH MARER-UTETE

dear fear, you can't have my ...

Dear fear,

Yes, I am unemployed. Yes, I am an orphan. Yes, I live in a country whose economy has been battered, bruised and brought to its knees. Yes, I do suffer from many ailments. No, I do not have it all or know it all. BUT NO! No fear, you can not have my influence. As God has promised me, my voice shall be heard among the nations, in every corner of the earth, across the borders and generations for many years to come. YES! God will increase my territory, my impact, my purpose. He will mold me into a woman of influence doing the work He called me to do. Like a restless sleeping giant, my great hunger awakens me. I have been disregarded, neglected, rejected, forsaken, forgotten and yet my creator has continued to raise me and hold my hand. I am not succumbing to you anymore, fear, because I have the Lord on my team. You can spare me the lies that I am not good enough. You can try to hold me back with your delaying tactics and distractions, but I know who I am and what I have been called to do.

I will brush off the dirt after you have hurled me down, pick myself up and move steadily forward with full intent and undeterred commitment. I will not pay heed to your loud reminders that I am without certain material things because I know that all my needs are met and all I need is God on my side to win my battles and conquer you forever. From this day forth, you are banished from my heart, my mind, my life. I am marching on to the promised land and leading the way for others who you led, like me, to believe that they can't or don't have what it takes.

Goodbye dear fear, your time is up!
Edith Marere-Utete

You Can't Have My Impact

Have you ever been so passionate about something that all you do is eat, think, sleep, dream about that one thing? That thing that keeps your adrenaline pumping and your senses excited? My thing has always been reading and writing. I enjoyed reading and writing more than I did going to play, watching television or chatting with friends. My imagination was always at its highest in these quiet me moments where I would delve into my own time and place. By the time I was eight years old I was telling everyone who cared to listen that one day I was going to have people reading a book or more written by me. I dreamt of the title, the cover, the launch even the book signing. Due to the fact that people do not always understand nor appreciate other people's dreams, I met a lot of discouragement, dismissal and ridicule. Can you relate to this scenario? When someone, particularly the people you love and respect try to sabotage your dream? Sometimes they do it unknowingly and other times they genuinely feel that they are saving you from some pain or disappointment. What this experience taught me is how unfair it is to undermine another person's dreams and I have tried as much as possible to support the dreams of others or at least give constructive criticism without crushing the dream in its entirety. Later on in life, when I thought I had the potential to venture into certain things that intrigued me such as becoming an engineer, a pilot or an astronaut, like clockwork I would convincingly talk myself out of it and re-focus on what I was conditioned to believe was my destiny by my naysayers. Whenever someone jeered at me, out of jealousy or simply because they misunderstood me, I would let that be my excuse for giving up on my goals and my interests. I became confused by trying to conform to the outside influences that told me I was a weak, good for nothing dreamer, and the internal fire that kept burning and spurring me on to do more and be more. I became constantly afraid of who I wanted to become and at the same time I was afraid of who I could never become – not in my circumstances, my community, my country, my poor, dark continent. Not with the colour of my skin, my social standing, my limited resources.

As I grew older, whenever I got the courage to write I would self sabotage myself and I would allow my fears to overwhelm and overtake me. I was afraid of being vulnerable, weak, of proving the prophets of my doom right. I was afraid of being in the public eye and under a heartless microscope. I was afraid that people would judge me and that my weaknesses would be exposed. I was afraid that I would be laughed at for not being good enough. I was afraid that people would not be interested in reading what I had to write and that I would negatively affect other areas of my life if I failed at this one. I was even afraid of what I imagined success would do to me. I would end up lonely, on some high pedestal that others would be unable to reach. My fear of success was compounded by the fact that as a high achiever I often felt secluded and disliked by my peers for being perceived as "the teacher's pet" or "the special child".

I remember once telling a friend about my vision and what I deemed to be my purpose and when her reaction was, "Wow! You're going to be famous!" I immediately cringed and pulled back. While I appreciated that my passion would possibly impact other people, that my vision had the potential to take me to other lands and to open me up to other cultures... I was filled with the dread of being exposed. I have always been a very private person and I was afraid of losing myself by unleashing my talents on the world. In order to counter unwanted attention I resolved to play small so as to avoid being too successful and "famous". I did not want to be an outcast and lonely. I wanted to fit in and be accepted. Success would create a bridge that the people I cared about would not be able to cross. I would make a lot of familiar people feel uncomfortable with my exposure and success. To top it all up, my culture and upbringing reminded me that success would expose me to enemies in the spiritual realm and I could end up putting my precious family at risk – of witchcraft, inexplicable misfortune or even death.

Being a modern African girl, I was caught in-between the superstitions and cultural pressures to be quiet and subservient and the global pressure to achieve higher qualifications and do better than the generations before mine. The world was getting smaller and more competitive so the pressure was on! Through it all I kept feeling the deep urge to share my stories and to let the world know that we are so similar despite our differences. I kept feeling the desire to be part of something greater than myself and to stop hiding my true God given talents, my passion and my purpose. I was not settled. I knew that I had to answer to God's instruction to share my story. Doing so would empower others and I would be able to find the release that I had been longing for, not to mention the fact that I would have fulfilled a life-long desire to be a positive influence, a voice for those who had been silenced for too long by culture, superstition, fear of the unknown.

My journey towards this realization started when I was suddenly unemployed in 2013, after serving in a socially enviable position. I was filled with the most dreaded fear of an uncertain economic future. I felt stripped, not just of my title, privileges and income, but of my self-worth and sheer confidence in my professional abilities. I did not take the "rejection" well because it was coming at a very bad time when the economy in our country was taking a downturn and unemployment was at an all time high. So the question that kept ringing in my head was what now? How was my family going to cope in such trying times? As I held on to my despair fear took advantage and moved in with me right there and then.

I felt more fearful as I compared myself to my friends, siblings, peers, competitors and even to complete strangers. I would look around at my peers and see all their academic, professional and personal accomplishments and I would tell myself that if only I had made time to improve my education, I might not be where I was. If only I had held my head down I might still have a job and an income. If only I had worked more on my personality to squarely fit my environment I would not have been cast out. The icing on the cake was that fear told me that I had no support system because my parents were no longer around to validate, comfort and strengthen me. I would apply for jobs holding onto the fear that I was not qualified enough, I was not experienced enough, I was not good enough. As expected nothing came out of the applications save for a LOT of gruelling interviews. Fear held me back from seeing that in spite of my reduced confidence, a LOT of potential employers found me to be interesting and worthy enough to be shortlisted and interviewed at all. Instead, I chose to focus on the rejection that came after this process rather than the lessons and exposure that I got from the preparation and experience.

With time I let go of the negativity and dwelt on God's promise that I will prosper and succeed in whatever I did. I just had to be strong and of good courage and to remember, as the scriptures said, to not be afraid or discouraged for the Lord my God would be with me wherever I went.

I then opted to learn from the experiences and successes of others but never look again at another woman with the kind of envy and comparison that distracts me from my own strengths and achievements. I am, after all, blessed with a high intellect, great personality, I am kind, compassionate and genuine in my love for humanity therefore my focus should be on these things that define my inner core and make me a unique and valuable member in God's incredible masterpiece. I do not have to keep waiting for the big and bold things to speak my truth, to be incredible and to make an impact. I am also under no pressure to please everyone all the time. I just have to be who God created me to be.

When I decided to heed God's call to tell my story a lot of opportunities came my way but I backed off time and time again. It was not until I decided to take action and challenge the mental, social and cultural barriers that were telling me that I was not worthy that I finally put pen to paper and poured my heart and my thoughts out. I shared my stories on different platforms and was astounded at the way that people responded to and related to my journey. It was a time of teaching and also of learning all that I had shelved inside me, a time of coming to terms with the pain and anger that I was holding onto that now held me back in so many ways. I learnt to confront my issues one at a time and even the unhealthy excess weight that I had gained over the painful, drama ridden years began to shed off, new opportunities began to emerge, new experiences and new encounters began to be explored. I found release and I touched more lives than I ever imagined.

Fear almost convinced me that my dream was not worth the effort, that my story was not worth sharing, that I could not financially, mentally and emotionally commit to breaking new ground. I had to crush the myths proclaiming that a job, a title, money were the only things that would see me making any positive impact in other people's lives especially those of my children. Fear had kept me thinking that my loved ones would not see the value of my decision to share my story, some people would despise my audacity, sharing my story would expose my vulnerabilities and negatively impact my chances of EVER getting a job or any income. Despite all this, as I challenged and overcame one fear after another I found peace, strength and contentment as well as sustenance, support and much more. As my friend aptly pointed out, "Ooh goodness I had so many fears and some of those fears were inherited or induced. But what I know now that I didn't know then is fear is not necessarily bad it depends on whether you use it against you or for you, whether you put it in front of you to stop you or put it behind you to propel you. Instead of asking what if I fail, I ask how many people would I have failed if I don't show up or become the best that I can be." I also learnt that even as I confronted my fear, it did not instantly and completely go away, fear just changed form and like struggle "it served a purpose, to help me dive deeper and draw out the next level of strength and become courageous."

As I evolve, when dealing with the fear of success I am encouraged to look at the example of Jesus who did not let the "fame" get in the way of His divine mission. Despite the positive and negative feedback He lived His mission and God's vision to the very end. His focus was not on the people and voices around Him but rather on what needed to be done. Jesus just DID! Simply and completely. But above all He did everything for the glory and honour of GOD!

My recent encounters and experiences have shown me that I am more than I or the world perceives. My experiences, positive and negative, have shaped me into the person that only God wants me to be. I have challenged so many strongholds and I continue to evolve in my journey to fearing less and rely on the promise and certainty that I can do all things through Christ who strengthens, empowers, inspires, encourages, uplifts, enables, comforts, elevates, sustains me. I have achieved so many things in my current settings and my situation which once seemed bleak and doomed. I have launched a non profit, created a lot of valuable content, spoken on many platforms, organized events and been involved in leadership roles that have impacted many. One lesson that I have learnt is that in the grand design of things, everything has a time and purpose. We may not understand nor appreciate why things are happening (or not happening) at the expected time but if we really dig deeper we will realize that there is a divine purpose in it all. God will make everything right at the right time. He will send divine connections that will help you when you stumble and hold you up when you get weary like Aaron held up Moses in the Bible. Remember that you are the light and salt of the earth therefore do not let anyone talk you out of your purpose and your dream. Allow God to lead you into your very bright, beautiful, impactful future!

Do you desire to make an impact in your network, family, community, country or even in the world? If so, how?

_____

_____

_____

How has fear held you back in the contribution to the well being and being of value to others?

_____

_____

_____

PURPOSE

BY TAREN KINEBREW

dear fear you can't have my ...

Dear fear,

You tried to immobilize me. I made a choice to come face to face with you and pursue my dreams in life and business. You have made every attempt to knock me off course. However, God told me I win. I decided to trust God on my path. With every step, I held his unchanging hand through every process. Although you may show up, I know that I can and I will push past you and decide to be the conqueror God told me I am!

Taren Kinebrew

You Can't Have My Purpose

My name is Taren Kinebrew, born and raised in Cincinnati, Ohio. I am a mom to one daughter, Brooke, and wife to Aaron of 18 years. We got married in July of 1999 after being best friends since high school. Our friendship was birthed out of a real love for one another. My career of choice is being the owner/CEO of Sweet Petit Desserts, which specializes in mini desserts. My passion and love for baking is my God-given gift, and I learned everything from my Grandmother Rose. She taught me many life lessons. Not until I decided to do this business did I realize my "why" and how fear showed up in different areas of my life. Please, let me explain.

My husband and I started out as friends, which really allowed us to understand and know one another. He is the one consistent male friend that I have had who gets me and allows me to be me. September of 1998 we connected, and out of nowhere my mom makes a statement to both of us that changed our lives. She said, "Sometimes love is staring you right in the face." We both looked at each other, and it was like the heavens opened up, like our eyes saw what they needed to see. Ever since that moment 19 years ago, we have been together.

I'm sure you're thinking what does my life have to do with fear? To be honest, fear almost kept me from my soulmate. This fear stems from not having my father in my life growing up. Actually, I have never seen nor met my father. So having a consistent male friend was the one thing I recognized in Aaron, and I wanted him to be part of my life even if it meant us just being friends. I just didn't want to cross of the line and end up with a failed intimate relationship. Quite honestly, the one thing that has kept us together for all these years, and even before, is that we have never had a screaming match. We've never purposely disrespected one another. Aaron is a very humble and respectful man and I have always appreciated that about him. He allows me to be who I am and really tries to understand the complexity of me changing over the years. We really work on having open and honest communication. Putting God first is the cornerstone of our relationship. We take loving one another as Christ loves us seriously.

My life is an adventure of sorts. I have made many career choices. I believe in living life to the fullest with what I am able to do. However, my journey has been based on my decisions, and not really influenced by one person. I grew up spending lots of time with my grandmother, who shaped me into a young person filled with God's love. However, not having a father in my life, as I mentioned before, left many voids. I only knew how a man should treat a woman from a woman's perspective. In my head, I always knew I wanted to be married to a good man who would be a great father, and I never wanted to be a mother without a husband. So in my journey through life, I saw healthy marriages from my friends who had both parents and always desired that. For many years, I had a hole in my heart because I just could not understand why my father didn't want to have a relationship with me. Not until many years later did I find out why my parents separated, and that my father simply wasn't willing to mend the relationship with my mom. He allowed bitterness to keep us all separated, including me. So, I was always in search of the guys who loved their moms and treated their families with the utmost respect. What I ultimately learned was that I ended up attracting men who had jealous tendencies, and their fathers were not active participants in their lives. To me, this showed their protective side toward their moms and any woman they cared deeply for. In my opinion, this caused insecurities within them that projected onto our relationship as a couple. The main theme was always, 'you cannot be friends with other men.' This really disturbed me because I was/am very comfortable in my own skin and I knew how to handle my relationships with men and even women. Ultimately, these types of relationships kept me off course in my purpose, which was to allow God to lead me and to have me build my relationship with him. I had to take a step back and do some real soul searching and understand the draw I had to this type of guy. It was basically familiarity, them also not having an active father. I stopped dating for months until Aaron and I came together in 1998. Prior to that, I had decided to focus on God. When I made that important decision, my eyes and heart were open to receive my husband.

Fast forward to 2008. I told my husband that I wanted to start a baking business. I had been asking God, *what is my purpose?* How do I reach your people and draw them to Christ? Since having the business, my husband has been by my side encouraging me, praying for me and ministering to me. Guess what happened next? FEAR came again trying to show me how inadequate I was and causing me to have roller coaster emotions! I learned through this to really trust God in my business and have the faith to let him take me where I needed to go. This didn't happen overnight. As a matter of fact, it was a long, hard process. The 3 things I learned were patience, perseverance, and purpose. God had to build these three characteristics in me, and while doing so, I had to have the faith to trust him through the process. There were many moments when I felt alone, even when I was with people, including my family. I literally felt like I was just surviving and having an outer body experience while running my business. I felt that Jesus was literally carrying me day to day. I was functioning as best as I could until I made the life-changing decision. *God, I will do what you tell me and have faith that you will do what I ask earnestly.*

What I would teach others, or better yet, say to someone experiencing challenges like this? Really draw close to God and keep the lines of communication open with your spouse. Learning how to have faith and trust God is truly a process. I look at my husband as a faith man, and let me tell you, he spoke life into me daily and prayed for me daily. It really helped and kept me focused for the most part. I just had to transform my mind by reading the word of God, speaking life to myself out loud and allowing it to get into my spirit. Upon doing so, I found myself stronger in God and in my Faith. Praying, fasting, and trusting the process also helped me combat the fear that would sneak up on me at times.

I am passionate about what I do because it's not just about feeding people naturally, but feeding people spiritually and helping them to believe in themselves. Things will happen, but you have to find the "why" within yourself! I help them to face their fear, and in spite of it, to push through. I encourage them to look at the bigger picture and not focus on the now. I get so many people that come to me asking, "How are you able to maintain your business and find balance between that and your marriage?" My answer is always, it's nothing but God. I am always seeking to flow in what God has put before me in all areas of my life. God blessed me with a husband in the natural and we are committed to one another. He has, at times, had more faith through our marriage and my business than I did. What I realize is that we both have faith and the only difference is that God met us both at our level of faith. I do believe that through our marriage my faith has surely increased because of the faith my husband projects and lives daily. This faith and belief in God has carried us both and grown us over the years, and it keeps getting better though it has its challenges. Having faith will always continue to stretch me because God wants me to continue to grow, which ultimately stretches my faith in him.

What keeps me motivated is knowing that no two days will look the same. I have grown to appreciate God for the simplest of things, like him keeping my mind in perfect peace as I grow in him. I work really hard at staying focused. I'm not perfect, but I do work at being honest with myself and my faith. It makes a difference when you know God will come through for you! So many times I have asked God to increase my faith in an area. At first it can seem a bit of a challenge, but it's amazing when you can see that your faith has increased in a particular area. I look forward to continuing to grow in God and increasing my faith however God leads me. The best part is that as I grow, I recognize fear and have the tools to combat it!

If I were to ever stop and not work in my purpose, which basically deals with matters of the heart and being an encourager to others, I believe God would be so disappointed in me. At this stage of my life, I care deeply what God thinks of the gift he has entrusted to me. I am the type of person who lives life with my glass half full. It's just in me to uplift and encourage others. This is what I do for me, my husband, my daughter, my friends, and for strangers, simply encourage and empower one to go forth. To me, not working in my purpose would be like not having air to breathe. In those moments when I have nothing to give, I retreat and get refueled. I have been too blessed and am still blessed with everything I've accomplished and I know that there is more to accomplish, which is basically God's work. In order for me to finish, I must continue to trust God, believe God, and have faith that God will see it through.

In my broken past, what I've learned is to give people grace. Grace is the freely given, unmerited favor and love of God. When someone hurt me, especially when I was young, I would have never given them grace, let alone forgiven them. What I am learning is that hurt people, hurt people and sometimes we have to take the time to just listen to a person and not react in a way that there is no room for grace. I've also learned to just listen to a person without judging. Judgements against people can be so harsh that if a person makes just one mistake we write them off. I did that often in my younger years, especially with my temperament. Now that I am wiser, although I may feel a certain way in some cases, I have to turn my mind off and just listen to the heart of the person; look past the emotion right in front of me and see through the pain. I also had to learn how to forgive people and give it to God. Unforgiveness and holding onto hurtful things can literally kill you. What I realized really early is that when someone wrongs you, it is better to forgive them so that you can live your life freely without the anger and the pain of a situation. I believe so much time is wasted on blaming others when things don't work out.

Throughout my years, I feel that I have learned some valuable lessons in regard to grace, being a listener, being judgmental and forgiveness. God teaches us not to be any of these things. I realize that people come from different places, backgrounds, ethnicities, and cultures and it's up to me to make the choice to be a vessel to be used by God. God has made no mistakes with me, so how he uses me is simply allowing me to comfort others through my gift of baking, pray for them through intercession, giving his people a word of encouragement, and speaking life into them and into the atmosphere. My husband and I operate out of love and our work is to bring people together. By me being a baker and sharing my love of baking, one of the ways that I exude love and bringing others together is by teaching those who have a desire to bake. The kitchen was my safe place and time where my grandmother and I had long conversations. She would sing praises to God and we would be the family I know people need in this day and time. Therefore, I use my kitchen to teach and empower others while listening to their story. So this is my story and I pray God speaks to your heart!

Dear Fear, you have taught me to live life more abundantly and to have faith in what God has shown me while not bowing down to you. My life is orchestrated and directed by God! I stand on God's promises for my life.

What is it about FEAR that is keeping you from moving

forward? Is it failure, intimidation, the unknown....

_____

_____

_____

_____

What is the BEST thing that can happen when you confront
FEAR?

_____

_____

_____

_____

SOBRIETY

BY PATRA SMITH

dear fear, you can't have my ...

Dear fear,

You had a tight grip on me, latching onto every part of my life. When I thought of facing a painful childhood memory, you were there, keeping me from healing and moving on. Whenever I thought of changing my current circumstance, you'd show up and remind me of how little I had to work with. And when I dared to dream about a brighter future, you would show up with your calculator to add up my past and present to remind me that I'll never amount to anything. You really had me cornered, and with your grips becoming increasingly tighter, I desperately searched for a relief from it all. I ultimately found that relief by finding temporary escape in an alcohol bottle. When I drank, it was only time you weren't there reminding me of my past, intensifying my less than idealistic present, and scaring me straight about what I wouldn't become in the future. Through my fear glasses, I viewed the comforts of alcohol as a friend when it was actually a well disguised enemy that was killing me slowly. I also couldn't see the alliance that you and alcohol had formed, with plans to keep me crippled and distant from my purpose. You two were seed stoppers! But now it's all clear to me! And you fear, have been exposed!

I've learned that fear is a blocker of purpose, so I've chosen to cut the hold you had on my life and press forward toward my purpose. Without you holding me back, I keep discovering new power within myself that I never knew I had. I was able to let go of the fake comfort I found in alcohol. Instead I found a new comforter called Christ, and together we water the seed that he has planted in me to help me flourish into the person he destined me to be. He said he had plans for me, plans to prosper me and to give me hope and a future exceedingly abundantly above ALL I could ever ask or think. Wow! So fear, you lied, but from now on you will no longer be able to contradict the truth of his words. Without you blocking my view, I can see things much clearer now. Good riddance.

Signed,
Patra Smith

You Can't Have My Sobriety

◆━━━━━━━━━━━━━━━━━━━━━━━━━━━━━◆

I was 18 years old, and freshly kicked out on my own.
Back then, my mom and I were in one argument after another,
never seeming to find the right words to reach common ground.
I was officially an adult and just wanted to be cut a little slack.
My mom was a strict island woman that had no tolerance for
two grown women living in her house. I wanted to be seen as the
woman I was growing into instead of being looked at as a little
girl that needed all these rules and restrictions. I just wanted
to be allowed a little freedom and for my voice to be heard, but
everything I said was considered back talk, so I held it all in.
My mom just wanted me to listen, do as she said and obey her
rules while I was under her roof, as she would put it. The tension
became very thick between us, and during one of our heated
telephone arguments she told me when I got home I would meet
my belongings packed and waiting for me to pick them up. She
said if I wanted to be an adult that lived by my own rules, to go
do it outside of her house. Right then, a strong feeling of fear
came over me because I knew I had nowhere to go, but my pride
kicked in and I said, "Okay," and went to pick up my things from
her house.

My girlfriend asked her mom if I could move in with
them. Her mom was nice enough to say yes, but once I got
there with my all bags, I quickly realized they had no room for
me. Staying there would have made everyone uncomfortable,
including myself. I knew I needed to find a place of my own, but
I also knew my job as a cashier at a smoothie bar wasn't going to

make moving out of my friends house a reality anytime soon. I was stuck between a rock and a hard place. I didn't know what to do, but I certainly didn't want to wallow in my new reality. I started going out anytime the opportunity presented itself, just to get my mind off of things.

While on the party scene, I was introduced to a new friend and we became close very quickly. I'd found a new friend that I could call on at anytime whenever a situation got tough or too heavy. Without the shield of being under my mom's roof, life was becoming too real too fast, so I was happy to make the acquaintance of such a dependable ally. She was a confidant, she never left me, she was the one I could lean on. I even gave my new found friend a name. I called her Enty! She was like gold in a bottle. Anytime I needed courage, I would have a few shots of her in a shot glass of Patron and I'd become like a lion. Anytime I needed to get away from the thoughts in my mind, I could have a few glasses of her in a vodka and cran mix and suddenly be on a hiatus. And any time I needed a good ole venting session, I could grab a whole Merlot bottle of her and have the best crying session, as if my good friend had stopped by to have girl talk. Enty was good to me. Whenever life seemed ugly and unbearable, she'd help paint a better picture for me. I had a one-stop shop in my new friend, Enty, and I felt as long as I had access to her I had a life long companion. She allowed me to escape my reality. I was afraid to see life as it was. Enty knew this and was good at taking me away. The more I spent time with Enty, the better I became at burying my truths.

I became very good at burying any thought that caused me pain. You see, I'd buried a secret that I had been holding most of my life. I had been molested at 10 years old. I was afraid to tell anyone, so I was left alone with the guilt and shame. I'd convinced myself that it must have been something I'd done to have brought it on myself. I also buried the fact that my heart ached every time I thought of the broken relationship I had with my mother. Sometimes I'd sit and imagine how great of a relationship we could have had if things hadn't turned out the way they did, but I just couldn't find the right way of communication to bring that fantasy to reality. We had become so distant over time, and unresolved hurt and unexpressed feelings drove a even bigger wedge between us. On top of all this, I was also constantly re-burying my current situation of being out in the world with no place to call home and no one I could call on. I was afraid to face all these things, so I buried them. And of course, Enty was there to help me disconnect from my feelings. Like magic, with every sip, they all seemed to become meaningless.

As time went on, I managed to find a new job and a place of my own to live. My friend Enty stayed close to me though, I'd become very good at hiding her presence. Our friendship had become seasoned, so we'd had some good times and some bad, like any other long term friendship. The more I aged and matured, I started to realize our good times were becoming far and few, and the bad times were more frequent. It was actually becoming my norm. I still didn't get rid of Enty though, because honestly I'd become accustomed to having her around. I felt dependent on our friendship. I feared losing her so much that I'd found myself trembling when I kept her away for to long. She'd been such a faithful, available friend to me over the years, so I had to be faithful to her too. Anytime she'd given me a night of fun and escape, I'd be required to pay her back by calling out of work the next morning, only to throw up, rest and restart, all because she still wanted to keep the party going. I lost job after job. She'd help me be a social butterfly on my nights out on the town. I'd meet nice friends, but then she'd require me to be distant and pull away from them to make more time for her. She was the jealous type, so I would eventually end up losing my friends. She'd help me through the tough times in my relationships, but then require me to get irate with them when they'd notice her presence. She didn't want to be noticed. Enty made me lose a lot, but at least I still had my trusty friend to comfort me and show me a beautiful mirage that everything was still ok, or at least I thought.

I started to feel our friendship took a turn for the worse and our exchanges were unfair. She'd help me bury my pain and escape for a night, and I'd have to pay her back with my jobs and my relationships. I thought, *What type of friend would be there for you, but in turn require you to pay them back with jobs and relationships?* But I feared walking away from what I thought was an old friend and comforter in hard times. I feared life without her because I feared feeling real emotions. I feared facing and dealing with childhood trauma, and I feared being present through the ups and downs on the roller coaster of this experience called life. Through my fear glasses, I wasn't able to see the truth; that the friend I ran to as a comforter was actually my worst enemy and was causing my downfall.

I started to come around to the truth that my so-called friend was actually holding me back rather than helping me along. I had to admit that Enty wasn't a friend, she was an addiction. And I, Patra, was an addict. So, I started to take some steps to make things better and take my strength back. I slowed down on drinking and I even attended some AA meetings. While sitting in an AA meeting, I realized I was the youngest person there. I sat there, afraid to share, so I just listened. I heard stories from people who had addictions older than I was. I heard stories of people having a long stretch of sobriety, but somehow falling off the wagon and ending up being sucked back into their addictions after 15 whole years of sobriety. Right then, fear took the microphone, tapped it to get my attention, then said loudly, "You see Patra, no matter how long you manage to stay sober, you'd still eventually be doomed from alcoholism." I sat there in fear thinking, *I just figured out exactly how I would die.* I got discouraged and felt like I needed a drink. I felt like running back to my old friend for comfort. Besides, it was hard to give up drinking completely, especially at my age, when everything seemed to revolve around drinking. Everywhere I went someone was offering me a drink, and it almost seemed to be a big let down if I declined it. I felt like I had a choice to either be housebound or a party pooping outcast if I went out and didn't drink. So I continued on in life with my frenemy, Enty, dragging her around like a ball and chain.

Who cares how I'd die anyway? No one would even notice if I was gone. I felt I had nothing or no one to live for. I struggled with being afraid to let go of something I knew was killing me, but held on to it because fear convinced me that it was all I had. Well, that was until I experienced hitting rock bottom. I'd been in a downward spiral of drinking for one week straight. I was polluted thoroughly with alcohol, there was no longer any pleasure left in drinking. It hurt me to keep drinking, but I knew it would hurt even more to stop. The thing that was poisoning me was also my self-prescribed prescription. Enty had loaned me her spirit to escape for a week, and as usual she wanted to collect her payback. But this time was different because she didn't seem to be asking for her normal trade. She wanted something much greater, and wouldn't settle for anything less. She wanted the ultimate form of payback! She wanted my life and my life's purpose! I felt it to my core, I was so sure of it! Enty, who disguised herself as my friend, was actually an entity on a mission to claim my life. I was sick and continuously throwing up. I had pain in every part of my body, all of my nerves were shot, I was weak and frail, and my mind was rambling with nonstop wicked thoughts. I was also seeing dark disturbing visions whenever I closed my eyes. I felt I was in a tug of war, as if something was trying to take over my body and get rid of me for good. I knew for sure I was wrestling with an entity for my life. I had nothing left in me to fight, so I knew if I was going to succeed at overcoming this entity, I needed strength that I did not have.

I didn't know what to do, but then I suddenly recalled a friend, a true friend. I started to cry because I realized how much space I'd allowed between us. I wondered if he'd forgive me for letting things go this far without reaching out to him sooner. I also began to remember his ways. I remembered that he was faithful and forgiving, merciful and compassionate. I remembered that he was all sufficient, especially in my weakness. I remembered that he was powerful and Almighty, and just what I needed. So I hesitated no further, and I called on him! With my polluted mind, I could barely get out a sensible sentence let alone a prayer, but I kept trying and with each prayer I sounded a little more sensible. I cried out for God. I asked for his forgiveness and asked that he save me! I thanked Jesus for the ransom he'd already paid for my sins and I asked him to cover my debt with the entity of alcohol that I'd abused for so many years. Through that prayer, I felt my slate was wiped clean and through God's saving grace I was no longer in debt to a spirit that wanted my life. That spirit would now have to face my God to get to me!

Although I was far from being out of the woods, I knew if I kept praying to God while keeping my faith I'd get there. In the midst of that fight, I saw clearly that Enty had stuck close to me all these years. She had been on a mission to claim my life, to stop the seed of purpose that God planted in me! But I was too fearful of letting go of something that had no good intentions for me. I realized right then, fear is the opposer of purpose! Fear is a well used tool by the enemy to stop purpose. While I reminisced on the motives of a fake friend, I had a epiphany! Through seeing the fueled determination Enty had to bring me down, it showed me the magnitude of my purpose. I became ignited by realizing that there must be something planted in me that is so grand and so praiseworthy that the enemy specially assigned Enty to ensure my purpose doesn't sprout. This realization made me value my life and the seed it carried. I started to see the light beyond the clouds. My mother took unauthorized time off work to be by my side. She was willing to lose everything else except me! All of the trying times throughout our relationship dissolved in the midst of seeing her love for me. Nothing else mattered except love. It was the key ingredient to bringing down all the walls of defense and miscommunication. My brother turned what was normally

4 hour drive from Tampa to Fort Lauderdale to a 2.5 hour drive, speeding to be by my side to make sure he wasn't going to lose his sister. He stuck by my side with no judgment, just pure love! And my love stuck by my side, neglecting everything else saying, " I can replace anything else I might lose, but I can't replace you!" Wow, that's love! I felt the love of family, love that fear convinced me I did not have.

That, combined with my new found value for God's purpose on my life, showed me I had a lot worth living for and a lot to fight for. I made a declaration to God and myself to never let fear control me again and to never devalue the valuable gift of my purpose that God designed just for me. I choose life over death and I choose to live in my calling! I've experienced what it's like to live in a poisoned, toxic body and how much of a prison it can be for the soul. A toxic mind and body serves as a blockage when trying to connect with God. It is a struggle for the soul to connect to its source while being encased in a polluted body. It is now my passionate mission to learn how to make the body and mind a perfect host to allow our soul to connect with God in a way that it allows us to be in perfect alignment to exude his spirit while we carry out his assigned purpose for our lives. I've been delivered from over a decade of an addiction and from the fear that fueled it. I know I don't look like what I've been through, but that just shows how good God is at restoring what we've lost and then some! God has blessed me with a thriving life 10 times better than what I could have ever imagined for myself. I live knowing that trials are sure to come, but through God we will overcome each one of our trial seasons! I've found blessings strategically planted in each one of the struggles I've faced, and as I overcame them, I received just what I needed to elevate in life. I know I am a better person having gone through them. Although fear has a job to do, my trust in the Lord will always supersede its efforts. And fear, in case you are wondering how I'm doing now, I live bountifully, pray combatively, think positively, speak peacefully, smile excessively, create powerfully, stand firmly, give abundantly, forgive thoughtlessly, love radically without boundaries, quit unwillingly, praise relentlessly, and pray unceasingly because I am blessed overwhelmingly!

What are some things in your past that you've buried and been afraid to face?
Once I became aware that the painful things I thought I'd buried were still resurfacing and affecting my current life choices, I knew I had to do something! First I shared with a trustworthy friend, then I sought further help with a therapist. I learned that carrying around old painful baggage can really weigh on you, even though you may think you've buried the memory. It can still be causing internal damage and can also be a blockage from advancement in life. Sharing is a vital healing tool that can give you the clarity you need to advance in life.

_____

_____

_____

_____

List 3 of your most common negative thoughts:

Once I discovered my negative thoughts were giving life to the fears that kept me restrained, I made a promise not to let a negative thought slip by without replacing it with a customized positive affirmation.

_____

_____

_____

_____

Write 3 powerful affirmations to directly combat those 3 thoughts you've just listed.

_____

_____

_____

_____

HEALTH

BY NIKKI MILLER

dear fear you can't have my ...my

Dear fear,

I declare that you no longer have residence in my life or the life of my legacy! You have been officially served an eviction notice, never to return! You no longer have the power to cause my past, my mistakes, my rejections, my grief, my hurt, my health, my pain and my depression to hinder me from walking freely into my God-ordained Purpose, Calling and Destiny!

Nikki Miller

You Can't Have My Health

Have you ever had a bad day? No, let me ask that question again. Have you ever had a really bad day? On December 8, 2010, I had the absolute WORST day of my life that changed me forever! My mother, sorority sister, best friend, rock and confidant passed away unexpectedly. I felt so lost and filled with lots of questions for God that I wanted answered immediately. I knew that I would never be able to live without my mother. I wanted to die. The months preceding my mom's death were slow preparation for what was to come, but I missed all of the signs.

In July 2010, my mother, aunt, daughters and I went on a cruise to the Bahamas to celebrate a few occasions; the completion of my Master's Degree in Education Administration, my older daughter's graduation from high school, and my younger daughter's 13th birthday. It was the most enjoyable and memorable experience with the most important ladies in my life. The first day on the ship, after we unpacked and began to take our first walk around, my mother walked very slowly and could not keep up with us. She finally broke down and cried and said that she needed a wheelchair. My mother had suffered with arthritis in her left knee for years and used that as her reason for needing extra assistance. On the day that we stopped in Nassau to spend the day, my aunt, my girls and I were so excited that we jumped off the ship so quickly, only to look behind and see my mother sitting on a bench. We just knew that she was on our heels. We all stopped and sighed. I felt myself becoming so upset. I could not believe that we were all getting ready to enjoy a day in

Nassau and mom was not keeping up with us. We went back to her and she was crying. She told us that she could not go with us. She could not walk the distance with us all day on the island. We were completely devastated. My aunt and I returned to the ship to ask if we could take the wheelchair off with us for the day. They agreed. We rejoiced, scooped mom up, and had a wonderful day.

My mom went to our sorority sister in October 2010, who was also our primary care physician, for a check up. At that appointment, she expressed to the doctor that she was experiencing shortness of breath, especially when walking. The doctor made a referral to a cardiologist to complete a stress test. Mom went to the appointment with the cardiologist alone. She failed the test. The cardiologist scheduled her to have a heart catheterization to determine if there was a possible blockage in her arteries that would potentially require the placements of stents. After this news, mom called all of our family together. The entire family began our own research on the heart catheterization procedure, stents, and other possibilities that might have taken place. I watched different videos on the catheterization procedure to learn what would happen to my mom. We talked with several medical professionals to explain how stents would be placed if she needed them, and the purpose. We invited one of our sorority sisters who worked as a Cardiologist Nurse for years over to my parents' house to walk us through the entire procedure and what to expect. As she began to talk, I felt so confident that mom was going to be just fine.

The day before the procedure, November 15, 2010, my mother's sister and my mother's brother arrived in our city to be with us for the next day's heart catheterization procedure. After having a family dinner, my mom's sister and I drove mom to the hospital where she had to stay overnight prior to the surgery. My aunt and I spent the night with her. We talked, watched television, laughed, and prayed. We did everything but slept. My mom was so anxious and nervous about the procedure. We had to request for the nurse to bring my mom some medication to relax her. After a certain hour, we all stopped talking and the room became silent. There was a stillness that filled the room.

On the morning of November 16, my dad and my uncle met us prior to the procedure at the Heart Institute. We had all of our family members cover my mother in prayer before the Heart Institute medical team took her back for her procedure. Each of us kissed mom and told her that she was in the best hands. We stood there and watched the medical team as they rolled her back, until we could no longer see her. All of us went to the cafeteria and ate breakfast. We were so certain that there were only going to be two results of the procedure; 1) mom would be fine and there would be no problems, or 2) she would need stents placed to open arteries. We had a beeper to let us know when to return to the family waiting area. One of our church members, who was a nurse at the Heart Institute, joined us. She was off that day and offered to sit with us and help us understand the results if we had questions. As we waited, the time seemed to go longer than anticipated, so our nurse friend went back to check on mom. She returned and told us that they were finishing and the doctor would be calling us back very shortly. I immediately asked her how mom was doing and how things looked. She said they were ending the anesthesia and getting her ready to meet us and the doctors. I thought, she didn't really answer my question, but

I knew my mom was just fine. Our beeper finally sounded and we were called back. Mom was sitting up in her bed, a bit groggy, but gave us all a smile as we entered her room. We told her how proud we were of her and couldn't wait to hear the good news from the doctors. She just smiled. Shortly after, several doctors entered with a big machine that had lots of graphics and results from mom's catheterization. The doctors introduced themselves and found out who each of us were in the room for privacy reasons. The doctor began giving us the results by showing us the graphics of mom's heart arteries, showing that she had severe heart disease with 90% and over blockage in all arteries. The only option was for her to have open heart bypass surgery. I just collapsed into the chair beside my mom's bed as I saw one tear begin to roll down my her cheek and the expressions on my aunt, uncle and dad's faces. I placed my head in my hands and just wept so my mom could not see me. This was not the news we were expecting. For the first time throughout this process since October, Fear met me head on! My family and I had lots of questions and were there at least two hours until everything was answered. Having talked previously with one of our sorors who worked at the Heart Institute for nearly 30 years, we immediately called her and gave her the news and asked her recommendation for my mom's surgeon. The Heart Institute checked the calendar and scheduled the surgery date for November 22, 2010.

The day arrived! On November 22, my dad and I took my mom to the Heart Institute for her open heart bypass surgery very early that morning. We stayed with her for all of the prep work prior to surgery. As always, before the medical team took her back, I anointed her and we prayed with her. I kissed her

on the forehead and told her that she was in the hands of the
Great Physician God Almighty who would heal her because
it was prophesied in Isaiah 53:5 NKJV, "But He was wounded
for our transgressions, He was bruised for our iniquities; The
chastisement for our peace was upon Him, and by His stripes
SHE was already healed!" She did not mumble a word. She
smiled and closed her eyes that were filled with tears. "I love you,
Mommy," were my last words. My dad knelt down, gave her a kiss
and said, "I love you, Mae." Dad and I walked away slowly toward
the family waiting room, where we would be until the doctors
completed the surgery. Waiting was so hard. I paced, prayed, and
listened to worship music. I called family and friends. I read my
Bible. It seemed to be the longest wait ever. Prior to the surgery,
the surgeon walked us through the entire process. I was sitting
there realizing that my mother's heart would be out of her body
for a period of time. A ventilator would be breathing for her.
Every time I felt a lump form in my throat, I just whispered a
prayer and read my Bible. Throughout the surgery, the medical
team came out to meet with Dad and I to give us updates. This
was very comforting. Mom did extremely well through every
phase. When we got the final notice that surgery was just about
over, I left my dad and told him I needed to go to the restroom. I
went in to be alone and I prayed like never before that God would
give me the strength to watch my mother on a ventilator and help
her come through the final part of the post surgery procedures.
My dad did not want to go back until she was completely awake.
He was afraid and did not want to see her in that state. The
medical team took me back by myself. A tear fell as I watched
my mother on the ventilator, connected to foreign machines and

tubes. The medical team was racing back and forth around her stabilizing her while weaning her from the ventilator. I stood and watched, shaking and praying. Fear hit me again, as I was so scared that mom was not going to come around. Finally, both of my mother's eyes opened so big. I remember raising my hands and praising God for allowing my mother to begin breathing on her own so quickly. At that time, I was directed by the medical team to say hello to her to encourage her to wake up fully. She was so very happy to see me. I told her how proud I was, that the doctors did an amazing job with her surgery and how she was on her way to recovery. Prior to her surgery, during a family meeting, my mom told each of us that she wanted this surgery behind her because she had a lifetime ahead to live. Mom was discharged a week later, and went home to recuperate with the help of a lot of family, sorors, church family, and friends. She was progressing pretty well, but it was a very slow recovery process. It was a painful process to watch my mother, who for all of her 64 years, had taken care of her parents, aunts, and other relatives, but never needed anyone taking care of her. She was such an independent lady of excellence, class, and elegance in every way. She was so well-known, loved and respected by so many from the full and fruitful life God bestowed upon her.

On Tuesday, December 7, I completed my work duties as an assistant principal at my elementary school, then went to my parents' house, as I had done every single day since she was discharged on November 29. A very special cousin who stayed daily with my mother was still at the house when I arrived. We did our normal preparation to help her get ready for bed that evening. For some unusual reason, my mother was very restless.

We would get her in bed, and she would want to get up. She was very anxious and agitated easily. She and my cousin began to sing one of my mother's favorite hymns, I prayed after they finished and we tucked her into bed.

On Wednesday, December 8, I was at school participating in an awards day assembly when I got a call on the radio from my secretary telling me I had an important phone call. When I got into the office, it was my dad on the phone. When I answered, he was crying and telling me that mom had stopped breathing and that the ambulance was on its way to the emergency room, and I needed to meet him there. My secretary drove me. After standing in the parking lot waiting for a bit, I finally saw the lights on the ambulance carrying my mother. My dad was following in his car. He parked and ran over to where I was standing. The medical team rolled my mom off the ambulance. She was connected to a mask and other things that I did not recognize. I ran over to her as the EMS men rolled her off the ambulance and started yelling, "Mommy, mommy," but they told me I had to go inside because they had to get her in quickly. The waiting room began to fill over capacity with family and friends. The news about my Mom being at the hospital had traveled all over the city, state, and country. This was my mother, who was known by all in so many sectors and capacities. After about an hour, the physician met with my dad and I and close family and friends to let us know that they were not able to bring her back after working on her for a long period of time. The doctor said, unfortunately, mom died. My dad and I just fell on each other, screamed and cried. Never in a million years did I think this was the news I would hear! What do you mean you worked on my mom and you couldn't bring her back? What do you mean my mother is dead? An enormous sense of fear hit me like a ton of bricks. How could I live without my mother? How would I tell my daughters that their Grammy had passed away? I could not believe this. I didn't want to believe it. After gaining some composure, the physician told us that it appeared my mother developed a blood clot post surgery that traveled to her lungs causing a pulmonary embolism. The doctor then told my dad and I that we could go back and see mom. Fear stared me dead in the face. I was so afraid. How could I see my mother dead? My dad, close family, and friends went back with us for a period of time.

When I saw her, she appeared to be asleep. I was still telling myself that my mom was not dead! She was alive! This was a mistake! I slowly walked up to her. I fell onto her warm body screaming, "Mom, come back! Please don't leave us like this! Wake up, mom!" She did not return. She did not respond. Reality finally hit me. My mother had transitioned from life to eternity. I gained a small speck of comfort when I noticed a smile on her face and the peace that I felt in her room. After what felt like a lifetime, we left mom and faced the aftermath - notifying family, friends, and dreadfully planning her funeral. The most difficult call that I had to make to inform of mom's passing was to her baby sister, my aunt. That was the hardest conversation. She and her husband came from their home immediately (five hours away) and helped Dad and I with all of the planning. My dad's house was filled everyday all day with family, friends, our sorority sisters, my dad's fraternity brothers, neighbors and church family. Everyone came from near and far, bringing us so much comfort and support.

The church was filled to capacity with those who came to say their final goodbye on December 12. Extra seating was placed around the sanctuary to accommodate all who attended, but many still had to stand outside in the foyer of the church. There were even people standing outside in the rain under umbrellas. This was my mother, and family and friends had come from everywhere to pay their final respects to this phenomenal lady. During the funeral, I recall sitting numbly on the front row with my family. I had so many different emotions. I was angry. I was sad. I was lonely. I was confused. I was in a fog. I was in disbelief. I was in denial. I feared living the rest of my life without my mom. I feared all of the special events that my mother would not be able to experience with us. I felt that God had made a big mistake. I didn't understand why He took my mother. I felt that He had forsaken me. Yes, I was very angry with God. As a part of our sorority's Omega Omega Service, I had to deliver the Eulogy. This was the singular hardest thing that I had ever done in my entire life. God's grace is sufficient and it was at this moment that I realized that God loves me unconditionally. He gave me supernatural strength that I didn't realize existed within me. I learned, even when we cannot trace God, we must trust Him!

My mother's death was mostly painful, but her death propelled me deeper into my purpose, plan and destiny ordained by God. In the days following mom's service, I had prayer warriors interceding for me because I could not utter words to God on my own. The scripture that was my mantra through this process was Psalm 30:5 AMP, "For His anger is but for a moment; His favor is for a lifetime. Weeping may endure for a night, but a shout of Joy comes in the morning." One of the hardest things that I had to deal with in the days after was helping my father process his feelings. He refused counseling. His way of coping was by visiting my mother's grave site every single day. After awhile, he decreased the visits to a few times a week, but even to this day, he visits her weekly. That's true love! Both of my daughters managed the process of this huge loss with such maturity, and they became a big source of strength for me. They are my two heartbeats who remind me daily of God's word, Psalm 118:17 KJV, "I shall not die, but live and declare the works of the Lord."

My grief was so intense. I masked it by pretending everything was okay. I tried to live my life "normally," but it didn't work. I found myself sinking into a deep pit of depression. I sought medical attention where I received prescription and therapy treatment. One of the most helpful sources was attending a group grief counseling series that Griefshare.org held at a local church. I also began subscribing to their daily email messages and purchased several books that assisted me. I became very active with the American Heart Association to educate myself on heart disease, the #1 killer of women in America. I participated in several yearly events including Heart Walks and The Red Dress Campaign. I educated my daughters and my aunt, and they joined me as advocates for sharing our knowledge, our story, to help other women understand the importance of ending this staggering statistic in our country. My sorority and other sororities supported me with my mission!

In December 2016, I began to have some startling health concerns of my own. I had an extreme increase in high blood pressure and even had to be hospitalized for monitoring and testing. My primary care physician referred me to a cardiologist for further treatment. The cardiologist, based on my mother's history and the symptoms I was presenting, immediately placed me on a heart monitor for a 30 day observation. At the end of those 30 days, I was diagnosed with Atrial Fibrillation (AFIB) - irregular heartbeats that can cause internal blood clots. He immediately began a prescription drug therapy. Additionally, he conducted two sleep studies, and discovered that I also had a mild case of sleep apnea for which I wear a CPAP every night. The one lesson that I learned from my mom's death was the importance of making my health a priority and helping other women to do the same. My doctor has me on a Ketogenic diet and a weekly exercise program for weight management to improve my overall health. Mom, I miss you dearly every single day, but your Legacy shall live on! Dear Fear, you can't have my health!

What are you current health concerns?

_____

_____

_____

What steps can you begin today to take control of your health and the health of your loved ones?

_____

_____

_____

dear fear, you can't have my

LIFE

BY SHERIKA JERNIGAN

...my

Dear fear,

I met you many years ago, at such a young age. I felt your presence hovering over my life. You made me feel like I needed someone to love me in order to live, that if no one loved me I was worthless and rejected. Fear, you planted this dark space in my head telling me I needed this person or that. You followed me everywhere I went. Your little voice tormented me for years. You isolated me from people. When I attempted to strive for greatness, you always took your best shot at me and scored. I could never finish that course and obtain that degree because you sat next to me. It took me a while to freely operate in my passion of dance to worship God because of your voice in my ear. You were whispering constantly, telling me, "You're not good enough! Who do you think you are? They're laughing at you! You look stupid!" You, fear, grew from a tropical storm in my life into a tsunami. I felt as if I was drowning, unable to survive and live. For the past 8 years, I've allowed you to control my life and keep me silent. You broke down my self-esteem.

I settled for a sore body, busted lips and black eyes. I tried to run from you, but tripped up every time. Fear, you really made me start to believe all the things you said to me were true. My life felt as if I was living in quicksand. I'm stuck, unmovable, and lost all because of you. Go away fear! My mind is tired of you. What do you want from me? I've allowed you to stay here far too long. I refuse to allow you to continue to walk next to me. I will finish strong! I will not allow another hand to be raised against me. I know who I'am. I'm moving your hand off my mouth. There's no more being silent. You can't have my story. You may be part of my past, but you can't dominate my future. I called you out and now I will conquer you.

Signed,
Sherika Jernigan

You Can't Have My Life

It all started twenty years ago. I'll never forget. I was only about five years old, in the back den of my mother's project apartment. My sister and brothers called my name, "Rika, there's someone upfront to see you." I walked up the seemingly endless concrete hallway. I didn't have a clue about who was waiting for me. So many thoughts flooded my mind. Who wants to see me? I'm just a little girl. Who am I to visit? I've never had company before. Is this a surprise? I turned the corner and a man stood there looking just like me and smiling. His smile was so big it lit up the room. I stared at him nonstop. The shape of our nose was identical. His eyes were glossy. I looked at every single angle and feature about him. He had hair like me. My stomach had butterflies and I felt so giddy inside. This man is just like me. It was my father standing in front of me. So many emotions aroused inside of me that I didn't know were there. I was so scared, but excited at the same time.

It's my daddy! I envisioned myself running and jumping into his arms. I saw myself hugging his neck super tight. All those things I wanted to do, but couldn't. My body stood there, frozen like a statue. My lips quivered trying to form words that just wouldn't come out. A small voice was saying, "Talk, say something," but I just couldn't. My heart was pounding so fast, racing like a marathon. Water began to fill my eyes and tears began to drop. I couldn't understand why I seemed so afraid of the man I was supposed to love, the number one guy that was supposed to protect me. He came to see his daughter. I felt so crazy because everything I wanted to do and say, I just couldn't. I stood there in complete silence crying. Fear was all over me at a young age. I had no reason to fear. But as I journeyed up the hallway, fear attached itself to me out of nowhere, allowing so many emotions and feelings to show that I never knew were even there. I was afraid, ashamed and timid. I had never experienced a moment like this. I was introduced to a word called "fear" that I wasn't even aware of. I didn't think anything of it; just a young girl having a scared moment. But little did I know, that four letter word "fear" had so much force and power. It was capable of doing things I never knew it could do.

Here I am, 21 years later having experienced the worst of fear. Something that seemed so simple at first was constantly challenging me and confronting me. It once took over my life without me even realizing, but I refused to allow fear to keep intimidating me. I'm finally about to face my fears. For years, fear stepped all over me. I allowed it to keep me in bondage in relationship after relationship; scared to walk away, scared to let go. I spent years being abused and many days accepting disrespect as if it was alright. I knew I was being done wrong, but I wouldn't accept it deep within. I was lost mentally. I didn't know who I was. I settled for less than I deserved to say I had a man. I didn't want to be alone. I wanted to be loved! I wanted to prove to the world and Facebook that I was the better woman. I used to cry myself to sleep from depression due to the mental, physical, and emotional abuse I endured. I would pack makeup under my eyes from fear of what people would say about me. I was dishonest to the people that cared for me the most. Fear stayed around me and kept my mouth closed. I used to tell myself it'll get better. I didn't understand what was happening to me. I started losing myself all at once. I felt lost, hopeless, insecure and worthless. I settled for anything just to keep my relationships. I crushed my self-esteem to feel wanted and loved. I simply didn't know what it felt like to be loved by a man. Something was missing in my life. I searched for it in relationship after relationship. It was like this thing called fear was controlling me. It just wouldn't leave me alone. It had turned me into a totally different person. I became bitter and angry all the time. My emotions were always everywhere. My mind was saying one thing and my heart was saying something totally different. I know I'm better than this. Why am I so scared to be alone? Why does it seem like I have to have a man? It's an empty void that I keep trying to fill. It's like I was fighting a losing battle. No relationship was working. I'm tired of trying. Maybe I need to stop looking? Why do I always end up in the same type of relationships? All those sweet nothings in my ear, and every time I thought the coast was clear. So many times I saw my way out of such brutal situations, but I found ways to stay every time.

But one day I got tired, and I was tired forreal. My body took all it could take. My mind was on the verge of losing it. My heart couldn't take anymore. This time I'm walking away and never looking back. This is not the life any woman should want to live; in fear, in a box afraid to break out. Fear really had me thinking love was supposed to hurt, that it was supposed to be hidden. I started believing that if I stayed, I could change them. I wasn't as tough as I thought I was. I was praying daily for better. I cried out to God to help me out of these situations. I had no more fight in me. I heard a voice one day that told me,

"You gone kill him or he gone kill you." There was a feeling that finally came over me of enough. I thought about that movie, and I most definitely didn't want to end my situation like that. I left! I got away! I began to go deeper in Christ. Church became my safe place. I would release my heavy heart and my confused mind every Sunday and cry out to God. I needed my life to be fixed, but I wasn't sure how. I got connected to the connection in the Kingdom. I gave God my yes and began to yield to the call on my life. Every Sunday and Wednesday, I began to let every word my pastor spoke marinate deep within. I started studying the word and wanting more of God. I was no longer looking for fulfillment in relationships with man, but only God himself. I chased after him like never before. I was empty and broken inside, so consumed with relationships that I strayed away from the person I needed the most, God. It caused me to be spiritually dead, mentally drained and emotionally ruined. I allowed relationships, man, and fear to pull me from the grounds I was raised on. I was determined to get my life, peace, and joy back. I was so tired of getting it wrong living my way. I wanted to live the life that God had for me. Yet I still felt stuck, and didn't know how to begin. What do I say? How do I fix this?

One evening at the Waffle House in Eufaula, I had a talk with Overseer Joel Parrish. I began to ask him how to get back right with God. I needed to get back on the right track. I feel the tug on my life. What do I do with this sudden feeling that has come over me? Is this for a moment or is God really calling for submission? I needed answers. Overseer Parrish told me to repent for my sins and instilled in me this prayer that said, "Lord, speak loud enough so I can hear you and clear enough that I understand you." That was an open invitation to show God that I needed him. I said that prayer every day. I even got it printed onto a shirt. I spoke it, I believed it, and I wore it. God indeed began to speak loud and clear. Through his manservant, my pastor, he spoke over my life about 4 times in a 2 month span, on the very thing I had been praying about and feeling. My life slowly started changing for the better. I had no control. A shift took place in my life, my mind, and I began to follow. I got so caught up in God's presence more and more each day. I could feel his Shekinah glory resting over me. It was a feeling I couldn't explain.

The love of God covered everything I had gone through. That void was no longer empty. I felt complete and started to feel like a new person. I found my happiness, peace, love, and joy all over again in Jesus. I knew then, that I had divorced fear and was marrying the anointing and call on my life. I wasn't scared of anything anymore. I didn't care about wanting a relationship anymore. I refused to settle for just anything. I wasn't scared to tell my story anymore. I no longer feared what anyone would say about me. I'm breaking every silent area in my life and freely operating in the will of God. My worship became deeper, and I started praying more. I ran to church every chance I got to get as much teaching as I could. I spent more time reading my Bible to know more about the word and Christ. I dealt with fear keeping me bound for all those years, but little did I know, it was only helping push me into my purpose and I rolled into my destiny. The shaking and the breaking in my life was all necessary. I am who I am today because God looked beyond my faults and met me right where I was. I began to do exactly what Matthew 6:33

said, "Seek ye first the kingdom of heaven and his righteousness shall be added unto you." No longer did I allow fear to make me feel ashamed, embarrassed, timid, silent or consumed in hurt again. My pastor, Apostle Paul Horn, spoke one Sunday saying, "Our hearts have so many hidden hurts and secrets that our mouths won't allow us to speak, and our minds won't allow us to rest." And that's how I knew that I still have more to share... To be continued...

Think to yourself, are you where you want to be with God? If not, name reasons why.

_____

_____

_____

_____

What are some ways that you can build a deeper relationship with God?

_____

_____

_____

_____

PASSION
PURPOSE & PROMISE
BY RHONDA GLOVER

dear fear, you can't have any...

Dear fear,

As I type this letter, I'm staring at the four corners of my computer screen contemplating what to share. I feel a little stalled as I push past the feelings that you have downloaded. You have had the ability to give me pause and stop me in my tracks. I want you to know that I see you. I see you lurking around, hovering, and doing all that you can do in keeping me from what God has for me.

Well, get ready. You are about to be deleted from my system. I have experienced you shutting down my thinking, but no more. I know I must look you straight in the eyes, like a fighter meeting his opponent in the ring. I am standing in front of you staring you down. While you are looking me in my eyes, I am dancing around in my head, pushing past all the shenanigans that you have conjured.

Fear, you are something else; showing up in the form of people discouraging me, making me feel like my desires mean nothing and telling me all that I want to do is a waste of time. What makes it so sad is these are the people who profess their love for me but really could care less about my aspirations and work overtime to ensure that I stay stuck where I am because that makes them feel awesome and special. Not anymore! I am looking directly in your eyes and saying, "HEY FEAR, I SEE

YOU!" I see you trying to slow me down, slow my roll and block my blessings. I see you trying to do your best in keeping me from what God has for me. But Fear, you need to know that my real Boss, my Heavenly Father, the King of Kings, the Lord of Lords has released me from your bondage.

Fear, you have been successful in silencing me from sharing ideas in the boardroom, the meeting room, and the classroom. I am reminded of Proverbs 4:25-27, which reads, "Let your eyes look straight ahead; fix your gaze directly before you. Give careful thought to the paths for your feet and be steadfast in all your ways. Do not turn to the right or the left; keep your foot from evil." God has my back no matter what. If I am standing tall, He is with me. If I fall, He is there to catch me. When I stall, He is there to nudge me in the direction I need to go.

Despite all your efforts, you need to know that you are messing with the daughter of the King. What God has for me will be for me, but I need to put in the work and push past you, Fear. I must remind myself every day that I need to stay the course despite how I may feel when you show up in my life.

Know this, God does not give me permission to give up. I must keep moving forward, persevering and be intentional about my walk. So, get out of my way and watch me as I stay the course. You have no place in my life anymore.

Rhonda M. Glover

You Can't Have My Passion, Purpose & Promise

◆━━━━━━━━━━━━━━━━━━━━━━━━━◆

CHECK THIS OUT, YOU FAILED TO KEEP ME FROM MY
PASSION, PURPOSE and PROMISE!

When I was a little girl, I was blessed to have my own
television in my room. Although it was black and white, it
served its purpose. With that black and white television I
religiously watched "The FBI" with Efrem Zimbalist, Jr. For
years I have tried to figure out what drew me to the show,
since no one introduced me to the series. I must take full
responsibility for that. I stumbled upon it as I sat on the
light green shaggy carpet that covered the floor of my room,
turning the knob to arrive to the channel of my choice. What
was funny about that was while I watched the show every
Sunday, I only remember one episode. It was about a little girl
who had been kidnapped, and the kidnappers kept her in a box
buried underground with a straw inserted in the box so she
could breathe. Well, that is how I remembered that episode,
and I am sticking to it.

Fast forward to 10th grade. I was hanging out with my
fellow cheerleaders in my high school guidance counselor's
office, and there I noticed a brochure on a book rack. It was
a recruiting brochure about careers in the FBI. I pointed
to it and said, "THAT'S IT!!!!" I am going to be a Special
Agent with the FBI. I did not waiver. I did not move. I was
unapologetic in my determination to become a Special Agent

with the FBI. I told myself I was going to become an FBI Special Agent over and over again.

I grabbed that brochure and what happened next was a blur. All I know I was forever changed. I had focus. I had something I was fixed on and determined to bring it to fruition. From that day forward, I was forever changed. That was it. Over the years, my friends from high school and college have reminded me how amazed they were that I knew my career goal. Without having the data to back it up, I knew there weren't that many black FBI Agents. This was a conclusion that I came to on my own.

After graduating from college, I was introduced to a family friend who suggested I get my foot in the door of the FBI. Working inside the FBI would position me to learn more about the Special Agent position. So, I did just that. I applied to the FBI! I submitted an application for the clerk typist position which required a typing test. I loved typing, so it seemed to be a great fit to get started. Although I loved to type, the typing test did not love me. I happily accepted a position as a clerk instead! I left the job I was in, and took a $6,000 pay cut to join the FBI. While it was a financial hit, I knew this was the best decision for me overall.

In August 1984, I reported for duty at FBI Headquarters as a clerk. I did not know where I would be assigned or what I would be doing but I was on my way to realizing my dream. Upon arrival, I was escorted to a large room that was donned with strategically placed flags to start my three-day orientation. I was still unaware of where I would be assigned. During the orientation, there were presentations on FBI history, structure, mission, and personnel matters such as benefits and time/attendance. Throughout the orientation, there were side conversations about people not wanting to be assigned to the Identification Division or Records Management Division. Back then, it was all about production in those divisions, and at that time, they lacked growth potential. On the third-day of orientation, we were told our assignments. I was told I would be assigned to the Technical Services Division. Someone told me that computers were in the Technical Services Division and it would be a good assignment. Straight talk no chaser, I was so full of myself! I knew without a shadow of a doubt I was on my way to utilize my "exemplary" computer skills. I was so excited! I was about to start my career with the FBI.

As I sat and waited for someone to escort me to my new desk, a woman walked in the room and walked toward me. She was fabulous looking for the early 80's. She was so gracious and welcoming. She wore a poofy skirt with a robust floral pattern, her make-up was impeccable, and she wore cat-rimmed glasses with rhinestones. We easily exchanged pleasantries as we walked through the FBI courtyard. She took me into a small conference room and welcomed me again to the FBI. She then proceeded to tell me that I was assigned to the FBI switchboard as a telephone operator... (pause for reaction and side-eye). I said, "The switchboard?" She said "Yes, the switchboard." I asked again for clarity, "The switchboard?" She repliued once again, "Yes, the switchboard." She then asked, "No one told you?" I said, "No." I felt my eyes well up with tears. Tears not flowing yet, but they felt like they were on the way. She was so sweet. She apologized because she saw how distraught I was. So many things were running through my head. What are my friends going to say? What is my family going to say? I can't tell anyone I am working on the switchboard as a telephone operator. I have my college degree. Surely this must be a mistake. I took a pay cut from my previous job to realize my dream which was quickly transitioning to a nightmare.

I fought back tears while being escorted to the switchboard area. As I walked in the room, I noticed to my right was a large switchboard reminiscent of the 1950's. She sat me down at a cluster of desks with large tan telephones. There were four round spindles that held panels with all the names of FBI personnel. My immediate task was to answer the phone saying "information" and provide contact information for FBI employees.

In between calls, I took a moment to call my mother as I continued to fight back the tears. I told my mother that I was assigned to the FBI's switchboard as a telephone operator. My mother proceeded to say, "Well, I guess someone heard your voice and thought you would be good on the switchboard." WOW! That right there gave me life, a new attitude. I was renewed and reinvigorated. Those 16 words took me to another level. The power of those 16 words changed my life. All of a sudden I started to sit straighter. At that moment, there was a shift in me. There was an immediate change in my mindset. It was like turning on the light in a dark place. From that day forward, I decided I was going to learn everything I could about the operations of the FBI switchboard.

When my attitude shifted, there was a shift in my thinking. There was a lot going on in the shift. I started to meet people at different levels within the FBI from the basement to the c-suite. I talked to the Director and other FBI senior executives daily, and in the process, became good friends with some high-ranking Bureau officials with whom I still maintain a relationship to this day. I quickly learned that the FBI Switchboard was the zenith of activity. Everything seemed to come through the switchboard.

Managers recognized my positive energy and drive, and I was soon encouraged to become a photographer in the FBI. I applied and was selected. Approximately a year later, I learned of another position of interest that became available. I applied, was selected and was transferred to New York City; one of my favorite cities! It was there that I officially took steps to realize my dream of becoming a Special Agent with the FBI. In September 1988, I took the oath of office as a Special Agent with the FBI.

Because I showed up differently, because my attitude changed, because I exhibited excellence, because I stepped up, doors started to open. Opportunities started to chase me down.

I want it to be known that you will have those switchboard moments where you will have to ask yourself how can I use this experience to get me to where I want to be? What do I need to do with this?

Well, you need to get ready to be ready, so opportunities can chase you down. Show up decent and in order and do your best in everything that you do. You don't know who is watching you or considering you for a position or promotion. Stay focused and do your best, and you too can experience the magic of the shift.

What dreams have you allowed to die on the vine?

_____

_____

_____

What blocks are you experiencing that are keeping you from where you want to be?

_____

_____

_____

What steps can you immediately take to move you in the direction you want to go?

_____

_____

_____

TIME

BY CARLA MCNEAL

dear fear, you can't have my ...

Dear fear,

Regardless of what you say, time is on my side. The Lord God Almighty, who holds time in His hands, is my strong tower. I run into Him and I am saved. He is the lover of my soul and the one who restores all. Yes, you told me I wasted time that I can never get back. Yes, you've woken me up at night with cold sweats and nightmares. And yes, you have whispered to me that I am a failure when I see others around me receive what I have been believing for. But as you plot and whisper while trying to attack and discredit my faith, I have resolved to shut you out by focusing on the word and my Redeemer whose sacrifice alone is my salvation. You have repeatedly dragged me down the dark hallways of my memory, reminding me of minutes, hours, days wasted in anger, frustration, and defeat. You've flashed scenes of my past in blinding technicolor, including the careless words that I spoke in Dolby Digital surround sound. But again, I've resolved to replace all of that with precious scripture, blocking you out by meditating on His love letter to me, reminding me that He is always doing a new thing (Isaiah 43:19.)

Instead of focusing on time lost, wished for, and waited on, I will REVEL in the here, now, and today. I will REJOICE in the blessings that He has given me. I will wait with ABUNDANT EXPECTATION, HOPE, and CONFIDENCE that the God who has supplied all of my needs, will continue to bless me regardless of my failures, regrets, and disappointments. As the sands of time flow, as the hands of the clock move, and as the days on the calendar advance, I have decided that you, fear, are no longer welcome in my life. This will always be the day that the Lord has made. And regardless of what happens, I will rejoice and be glad in it.

Fearlessly,
 Dr. Carla McNeal

You Can't Have My Time

◆━━━━━━━━━━━━━━━━━━━━━━━━━━━━━━◆

"For the vision is yet for an appointed time, but at the end it shall speak, and not lie: though it tarry, wait for it; because it will surely come, it will not tarry."- Habakkuk 2:3

As you have come against me to remind me of what I don't have and cannot control, I am learning to enjoy my right now as I wait for time to reveal, not necessarily what I desire, but what God has planned. To combat your lies, I've developed something that I will use to take my mind away from time and instead help me focus on how I can, in fact, praise God in that hallway until the next door opens.

W-Watch for God's hand in seemingly insignificant things. Doing so reminds me that He is there and working in my favor.
A-Attend to what God has given me: my family, my talents, my profession, my relationships. Spend my time nurturing these blessings.
I-Inspect my attitude at all times. Am I grateful, thankful and faithful? Am I worried, frustrated? I should be aware of every response to every situation.
T-Testify to myself to remind myself of what God has already done in my life. Remember Clay Evans' song, "I've Got a Testimony?" "When I look back over my life, and I think things over. I can truly say that I've been blessed, I have a testimony."

You no longer cause me anxiety or panic. You can no longer choke or paralyze me. Fear, you're on notice: your time is up.

****

Sometimes, I think about my life in analogies of songs because I am a singer. If fear were to sing a song to me, it would go something like this: "Do you remembah…the 16th and 23rd of Septembah?"

September 16, 2013 started out as a normal day. It was a Monday, still relatively warm even though those of us in the DMV area (D.C., Maryland, Virginia) were hoping for early signs of fall. I was in my first year as an assistant principal, and that morning at about 8:15, we were ending our weekly calendar meeting. My mind was elsewhere. My husband of five years, Cedric, and I were in the middle of marriage counseling, and the sessions did not seem to be getting us anywhere.

Once I got back to my desk, my cell phone pinged with a text message. It was Cedric. The text read, "Someone just came into my building and started shooting." This was the onset of what we now know as the Navy Yard Shooting. My husband worked in the NAVSEA Building 197. I had gone there the year before to attend his promotion ceremony. I quickly started searching the internet for news because I was calling Cedric, but not getting an answer. It had literally just happened, so the news outlets hadn't even picked up the story yet. I started thinking about the time with him that I had taken for granted. My memory's museum began to show me exhibits of my selfishness toward him. I became nauseated. Immediately, I began to pray. September 23, 2014 started out just as normally. It was a Tuesday morning, and it actually was cooler than normal; fall was imminent. I was still an assistant principal at the same school. I wore a kelly green Kasper blazer that morning, and I remember one of the teachers commenting on how pretty it was. Once the day had started and students were in class, I settled at my desk. One of my resource teachers was in my office talking to me about something, and as we were wrapping up, my cell phone rang. I saw it was my Daddy. As soon as I heard his voice, I knew. My precious 80-year-old grandmother, who was as constant a force in my life as the sun itself, was gone. We didn't even know about her illness until the previous May. I fell to my knees in tears, and I started replaying the last time I saw her in my mind. The exhibit in this part of the museum was hard to swallow.

It was Christmas 2013. We were at her house in rural Alabama. As she had ten children, there are a lot of us, so the house was packed. We'd eaten, talked about the Iron Bowl, and shared typical family jokes. One of my aunts, who lived in Virginia, did not make the trip, but called to speak to everyone to wish them a Merry Christmas. When she wanted to talk to me, my grandmama tried to hand me the phone, but I declined. You see, I had been in the DMV since 2011, and this aunt never attempted to call me or come and see me, so me and my silly self was a bit indignant toward her. My grandmama got me told in good old down South grandmama fashion, "Stop acting so silly and being so mean. Why you don't want to talk to her? Seek peace and pursue it!" Although I talked to mama (what I called her) many times after that, I was sad that the last time she interacted with me physically was by chastising me to be decent to family.

Because of the infinite grace of God, the covering of His Son's blood, and the hovering of angels, Cedric was protected during the shooting. He walked away physically unscathed, although the mental and emotional tolls were great, as he lost a very close colleague. The next session of counseling we had, we walked in and told the counselor that we no longer needed his services. There was something about the possibility of loss that sobered us. The same was true when I lost my grandmother. In a way, time became more precious to me, while simultaneously becoming one of my most antagonistic foes.

After these two experiences, I came face to face with a real anxiety that I struggle with to this day: a fear of the unknown, a fear of what I cannot control, a fear of the "what ifs", a fear of what is on the other side of this phone call. It's suffocating, debilitating, and paralyzing. Maybe everyone deals with this, but what this fear highlights for me is that I cannot control time, and that stresses me out.

The first time I had a real panic attack, I was lying in my bed attempting to go to sleep. I realized that I was a few years away from turning 40. Even now, my heart skips a beat thinking about the fear that gripped me, the way my breath caught in my throat, and the way the walls seemed to close in on me. I sat straight up in my bed as all of the blood rushed from my head and the tears choked me. The reason I was so shook was because there was a voice in my head screaming at me, reminding me of my age and how there were so many pieces of my life that were still missing. The uncertainty of my tomorrows made me feel completely out of control.

The second time, the feeling was similar, but the root of the panic was a bit different. I realized that my parents were getting older. The awareness of it made me want to scream. It may seem insignificant to some, as parents aging is just a part of life. But the reality is, most people don't think about their parents aging until they actually start, and my parents are a huge part of my life. The thought wrapped me in a suffocating blanket of fear as I grasped this inescapable fact. I spiraled down and couldn't breathe, and again, the uncertainty glared at me.

Early in their career, the Christian rap group D.C. Talk had a song called "Time Is," and the hook went like this: "Time is ticking away, tick tick ticking away. TIME is ticking away, tick tick ticking away." When I think about all of the time I wasted arguing with my husband over silly things or when I didn't value the time I spent with my grandmother, I have regrets. On the other side of that coin, however, is the very stark reality that I am not getting younger and this life isn't a rehearsal; this is the only one I get. I start thinking of mistakes I made and time I wasted on ridiculous things and people. My mind wanders down rabbit trails. Wonder what would have happened if I had done this, gone to that college, moved to that town, taken that job? The irony is that as the enemy takes me down those rabbit trails, he is distracting me from now and today and helping me to waste even more time!

In terms of time, I think about the three nuances that are most poignant for me: 1) I feel like I've wasted a lot of time; 2) I feel like time is moving too quickly; 3) I also feel like time isn't moving fast enough. Let me clarify. When it comes to the promises that I believe God will fulfill in my life, I'm impatient, feeling that I shouldn't have to wait (especially if it LOOKS like others around me didn't have to wait). On the other hand, when I think about how old I am and where I am in terms of the goals that I have for myself, I wish time would slow down so that I can reach those goals. Confusing, I know. Welcome to my world.

We've heard the cliché, "While you're waiting on God to open the next door, praise Him in the hallway." I sincerely wonder if people who say and believe that have actually experienced what it is like to see everyone around you have things happen for them (seemingly) without struggle or wait. I sincerely wonder if people who say and believe that can honestly attest that waiting is an experience that can actually elicit praise. God is not bound by space nor time. But, in His infinite wisdom, He can use every one of our experiences for His glory. Jeremiah 1:5 says, "Before I formed you in the womb I knew you, before you were born I set you apart; I appointed you." Knowing us before we were born transcends beyond finite time constraints as we know it. And if God wrote in His Word that He has already set me apart and appointed me, why do I worry so much about time?

My favorite season of the year is fall, hands down. The colors of the leaves take my breath away. But a close second would be spring, because after a dead, gray winter, I have to admit that the greens, pinks, yellows, and purples that accompany the vernal equinox are beautiful. A few weeks ago, Cedric and I were driving into D.C. for a retirement ceremony. I complained that it was mid-April, but the leaves on the trees had yet to appear. This morning, literally two weeks later, I drove the same route to accompany my students on a field trip and was amazed at the greenery that had emerged! When the leaves fall off of trees in autumn, the trees don't get mad and start questioning God about when their leaves are going to come back. They don't complain about time. They stand there, in their dormant season with their limbs lifted in praise to God. They know that their Creator, the One who suspended the very earth in space, the One who can number the hairs on our head, the One who knows the end from the beginning will cause their leaves to return by awakening their internal clocks when it's time. It happens almost imperceptibly.

You see, my 16th and 23rd of September caused me to think a lot about time: time lost, time desired, time wished for, time expected. Those two days also made me think about what I want and don't have. If you're of my generation, you remember the movie "Willy Wonka and the Chocolate Factory." You also probably remember one of the more infamous characters, Veruca Salt. Veruca was a spoiled brat who got everything she wanted when she wanted it. She even sang a song called, "I Want It Now." The lyrics said, "I want today, I want tomorrow. Don't care how, I want it now." Sometimes I feel like Veruca. Sometimes, I just want what I want when I want it. And although I'm beyond questioning God, I am still learning the art of waiting and the beauty of His perfect will.

I know I am not the only one who has gone to bed at night sobbing into a pillow wondering, "How long will I have to wait? How long do I have to live with this pain? How long do I have to go without an answer? When? When? WHEN?" The thing is, we can ask these questions all we want, but the answers still evade us. So, we try to remain faithful and hopeful because hope does not disappoint (Romans 5:5). Meanwhile, standing in that hallway gets more frustrating, more challenging, more worrisome. The hands of the clock tick.

Consider the time between the First Adam and the Second Adam; we're talking about thousands of years. Israel prayed endlessly for a king, for a redeemer. Isaiah prophesied about Jesus some 700 years before He was even born. And God was faithful. In His time, He sent our Savior. He fulfilled His redemption plan to His creation.

I often make the analogy that our lives are like tapestries that God weaves using experiences, trials, and victories. One day, I looked up what it takes to make a tapestry and how long. I learned that it takes about two months, but that's for a skilled person who spends at least 35-40 hours per week at the loom. The individual uses various colors of yarns to make intricate patterns that reflect beauty and skill. We are blessed to be children of the master Tapestry Artist. Our lives, even the difficult waiting seasons or seasons tinged with regret and worry, reflect His ability to use the colors that we may not appreciate in ways we never imagined.

There is the saying that "time waits for no man." This is true, but praise the Lord, I am infinitely blessed because the author of my life has placed His favor on me and every part of my life regardless of time! And whether I feel like I've wasted time, time is going too quickly, or time is going too slowly, He has promised to give me beauty for ashes, oil of joy for mourning, and a garment of praise for the spirit of heaviness. All of these things being residuals from my love-hate relationship with time. He still makes all things new, and will continue to do new things...in His time.

How would you describe your relationship with time? Do you struggle with wasting time, wishing time would slow down, or wishing time would speed up? How can you reconcile these conflicts within yourself?

_____

_____

_____

_____

Think of your biggest regret and how you think it may have cost you time. Consider how God has used that regret and seeming waste of time for His glory and your benefit. If you're struggling to do so, read Joel 2:25 and Isaiah 61:1-4, and see that God is a God of restoration. Write your own declaration of His restoration for you.

_____

_____

_____

_____

Meet the Authors

Tyecia Powell

Tyecia Powell is the Regional Director of Bikram Yoga Works and works with kids and adults in the community to change bodies, minds, and lives through mental health and wellness. Tyecia is a native Baltimorean who believes that change starts at the root. Tyecia has worked in public schools for over ten years as a teacher, academic coach, and most recently as an Assistant Director of Urban Teachers, an alternative teaching certification program. Through these various roles, she has always strived to foster growth and development in everyone she encountered. Tyecia is a trained Pilates, CPR, and Mental Health & Wellness Instructor, as well as a trained basketball, softball, and track coach. She is a lifelong learner holding a Bachelor's Degree in English and Education (UMBC), a Masters Degree in Teacher Leadership (Valdosta State), a Specialist Degree in Leadership (Walden University), and is currently working on her Educational Doctorate in Leadership & Management (St. Thomas University).

Tywauna Wilson
"Coach Tee Wilson"

Tywauna Wilson has been deemed a leader to know within her local community and her profession. She is the owner of Trendy Elite, LLC which she founded in 2017. Trendy Elite is a consulting firm that focuses on transformational leadership by equipping rising stars with the tools and expertise needed to be successful influencers who inspire personal growth and progressive success in the workplace and in their local communities. Trendy Elite offers a variety of training programs, leadership assessments, coaching, and mentorship programs for both adult and teens. Tywauna has received certification by leadership guru John Maxwell and his team and utilizes their proven curriculum in some of the Trendy Elite training programs. Trendy Elite is committed to creating a pipeline of successful leaders who add value to their organizations and the people they serve in the community.

Prior to starting Trendy Elite, Tywauna, spent the last 14 years in a variety of progressive leadership roles in the clinical laboratory working in both hospital and reference laboratory settings. She currently serves as the System Technical Director of Chemistry at one of the top regional laboratories in the Greater Dayton community where she provides clinical chemistry expertise to six hospital sites and a core laboratory facility.
Mrs. Wilson holds a bachelor's degree in Clinical Laboratory Sciences from Kentucky State University and a MBA from Indiana Wesleyan University. She received several awards and

honors, including: 2017 American Society of Clinical Pathology Forty Under 40 Award, 2015 UC/UC Health Martin Luther King Jr Honoree, 2012 Girls Scouts of Southwest Ohio: Celebrating a Century of Service Leaders of Promise Award, 2011 Cincinnati Business Courier Forty under 40 Award, and 2010 YWCA Rising Star.

Tywauna is actively involved in the Urban League of Greater Southwestern Ohio, Cincinnati Alumnae Chapter of Delta Sigma Theta Sorority, Inc., American Society of Clinical Pathology, Cincinnati Kentucky State University Alumni Chapter, The John Maxwell Team, The Dayton Public Schools Foundation Board, and the National and Cincinnati Board of Realtors.

Tywauna lives in Cincinnati, OH with her loving husband, Martinez, and is the stepmother to three wonderful kids. When she is not spending time with family and friends, she enjoys reading, traveling, engaging in fitness related activities, and living life likes it golden!

For booking information or to schedule coaching/training:
Website: www.trendyelitellc.com
Email: tywauna@trendyelitellc.com

Anita King Jones

Anita King Jones is an ordained Evangelist; she's a wife, a mother, and a grandmother. She obtained a Masters of Pastoral Counseling from Andersonville Theological Seminary in Camilla, Georgia. Although her profession is a Bookkeeper, the opportunity often presents itself to be a counselor even in the office. She declares that 'prayer is her weapon'. She seeks God's will for growth through the obedience of His word. Although she went through a period of life's unfavorable circumstances, she is a firm believer that God was working in her favor to build faith in Him. She now is an advocate for hurting women. She is an exhorter and an encourager, a counselor and a teacher. She is well qualified to testify that God is a protector and a deliverer. God has engraved in her heart the ministry of forgiveness. By the power of God's anointing, she lives to break the yoke of bondage in the lives of women who have been mentally and physically abused.

Ashley Little

Ashley Little is a strong leader who has a passion for changing lives through education. She has been working in the for-profit education field for over 13 years. She has held many different leadership positions and she loves being able to help students who might not have the opportunity to attend a four year college continue to be successful. Ms. Little is an aspiring entrepreneur who loves empowering women in many different walks of life build confidence emotionally, mentally, and spiritually through public speaking.

Next, Ms. Little is a WomanSpeak Circle Leader Business Owner. She teaches women how to be more confident in every area of life through public speaking. She teaches them how to be more confident in their abilities to speak up and have a voice. She takes pride in helping women share their voices and deepen their leadership.

She is a proud member of Delta Sigma Theta Sorority Incorporated and a member of Alpha Phi Omega. She is very involved in her community, organizations and non-profits. Currently, she is one of the founders of "The Sweetheart Scholars Scholarship" along with three other powerful women. This scholarship will be given to two Aspiring African American Females from her hometown of Wadesboro, North Carolina who are attending college to help with their expenses. Ms. Little believes it takes a village to raise a child and to never forget where you come from. Ms. Little is a strong believer in giving back to her community. She believes our young ladies need vision, direction, and strong mentorship.

Furthermore, she is a ForEX Business Owner where she teaches people how to trade foreign currencies and achieve financial freedom through investing. She loves being able to bless other people's lives by helping them get to the next level in their finances. She believes Financial Freedom and Retirement is something we all want and need.

Ms. Little received her undergraduate degree in English from North Carolina A&T State University. Next, she received her Master's Degree in Industrial Organizational Psychology. Ms. Little is a mover and shaker and she continuously pushes herself to be better than she was yesterday. She gives GOD all the credit for everything that has happened in her life. She has strong faith and determination to be great. She believes her only competition is herself. Her favorite scripture is Philippians 4:13 "I can do all things through Christ who strengthens me".

Yvonne Mtengwa

Yvonne C. Mtengwa is the author of "Reinvented: Challenging insecurity to live authentically through faith", a book encouraging women to confront their issues with relationships, insecurities and self-fulfilling prophesies, in an effort to truly discover who they were created to be.

Passionate about travelling, writing about and experiencing leisure and lifestyle brands, Yvonne is a marketing and communications strategist, and is also the Co-founder of Quintessentialf.com, a Christian lifestyle movement for women. Through this platform, she continues to garner acclaim as a speaker and motivational blogger with messaging that targets the millennial African woman.

Yvonne is also the Founder of Narratives Inc., a boutique communications agency specializing in entrepreneurial design and shaping the narrative of lifestyle and social development enterprises across sub-Saharan Africa.

She is wife to Bernard and mother to two children Shalom and Ithai.

To read more about Yvonne, visit her website on www.ReinventedToday.com

Shani Farmer

Shani Farmer is an aspiring entrepreneur with a passion for helping women express themselves freely while cultivating self-love, spiritual growth and personal empowerment. Mrs. Farmer embodies the ideals of sisterhood and service for others which solidified her decision to become a member of the illustrious sisterhood of Delta Sigma Theta Sorority Incorporated while attending North Carolina Agriculture and Technical State University. This is where her truths and her passion were fully manifested; she has been able to serve on boards for at-risk youth with a focus being on mentoring young girls in her surrounding communities. She currently volunteers her time by helping students excel in interview preparation for private school acceptance. She has created an easily executable curriculum to equip students with the necessary foundational knowledge, etiquette and confidence to successfully navigate the interviewing arena.

Mrs. Farmer received her undergraduate degree in business management and pursued her MBA with a focus in entrepreneurship. She was blessed at an early age to add critical real world experience to her collegiate education with her first career opportunity being at the Ritz Carlton Orlando. She served as a concierge and through her experiences and substantial responsibilities at such a prestigious corporation, Mrs. Farmer began to carry herself with the company brand from that day forward, "The Gold Standard". She turned the lessons from that time in her life into an 8+ year career at the Department of Defense as a Human Resource Specialist with a focus on Employee Relations. In her current position, Mrs. Farmer takes a prominent role in the advising and mediation of issues, disputes and violations that adversely affect relations between senior level leadership and Agency employees. She is very much driven in her current place of employment but it is to be noted that the never-ending desire of entrepreneurship she has in her heart will never fade. Mrs. Farmer recently became a home-based business owner as a Romance Consultant for "Pure Romance". She takes pride in being able to educate, empower and entertain wives and brides to be across the country; teaching countless women to love themselves and how to create a healthy space of love between them and their spouse. Her vision is to build up a network of women in different stages of their lives and provide products and services that will inspire them through the essence of beauty, faith and power.

Mrs. Farmer is a newlywed and has dedicated her love and support to her go-getter husband Benjamin Farmer. She is a native of Buffalo, New York and has lived in Orlando, Florida and Greensboro, North Carolina. Her unwavering faith and determination to never quit has brought her to this place of Gods ordained plan for her life. Join her on this journey to freedom and watch her WERK!

Chinita Irby

Chinita Irby is the mother of a handsome son, Dewan Jr. and an elementary school instructional leader. She served as assistant principal, and an elementary school instructor. Chinita holds a M. Ed. Elementary Education and M. Ed. Instructional Leadership. She has served as a certified Online Rater for Education Testing Service. Her professional experiences include, but are not limited to, member of Delta Sigma Theta Incorporated, Delta Teacher Efficacy Academy, Alabama Education Association, Alabama Education Association Delegate, past Vice-President of Dallas County Professional Education Support Association, Optimist International, Order of Eastern Star Salem Pride Chapter #509, Association for Middle Level Education, 2016-2017 CLAS Professional Development Council , Gear Up Alabama Technical Assistance Team, AdvancED Engagement Review Team Member, and AdvancED Engagement Review Associate Lead Evaluator.

Christine Handy

In her career span, Dr. Christine Handy has always been in a helping or coaching role. With more than 30 years as teacher, track coach and high school principal, while an entrepreneur, Christine's life mission is to enhance the life of others via education, counseling, and coaching.

Christine has enjoyed an amazing 30-year career in the field of education. She started as a Special Education teacher and has served as a high school principal for the past 19 years. Christine was recognized as the 2006 State of Maryland Secondary Schools Principal of the Year and was the 2014 recipient of the prestigious Dr. Edward Shirley Award for Excellence in School Leadership. A respected leader in education, she begins her term as President of the National Association of Secondary School Principals in July 2018. She is especially proud that 8 school leaders that she has mentored have been promoted to school principal positions. Christine is an international speaker and trainer. She has trained school leaders in Beijing, China and across the USA at Equity Colloquiums, National College Board, Advanced Placement and National Principals Conferences. She is also a trainer, coach, and speaker with the John Maxwell Group, specializing in presentations on "Leadership Matters" and leading teams through The Leadership Game. She loves helping others develop their leadership skills, grow their business, and to realize their financial dreams. She also specializes in supporting our youth through presentations and workshops at youth retreats and summits. Christine is also a member of Delta Sigma Theta Sorority. She is a proud entrepreneur. For the past six years she has been involved with Send Out Cards, a technology based company that uses a mobile platform to support businesses and individuals with Relationship Marketing and increasing repeat and referral business by sending greeting cards and gifts in the mail. A leader, Christine was selected to serve on the Eagles Nest amongst the top earners with the company and her current rank is Senior Manager.

You may reach Christine at christine@everyoneloves.cards or success@aboveonly.ws

<u>Follow her on Social Media</u>
Facebook - www.facebook.com/chandy18 or
www.facebook.com/christinethecardlady/
Instagram - www.instagram.com/christine_the_card_lady/

B. Jacqueline Jeter

B. Jacqueline Jeter aka The Encouragement Ambassador is a celebrated Independent Certified Leadership Coach, Teacher and Speaker with The John Maxwell Team. She uses her platform as a published co-author in the best selling anthology, Endurance: Going the Distance From the Valley to the Mountaintop, and as the Visionary of the encouragement blog, Reign Drops, to further her mission of helping others see that no matter what they are facing they can walk in triumph. Her motto is Triumph trumps winning....every time.

Jacqueline is also the CEO and Founder of the personal development company, The Ripple Effect Development Group, whose passion is to empower women of all walks of life to realize their full potential and excel in their life's passion and purpose.

In conjunction to leadership development, Jacqueline is a consummate pharmaceutical veteran with 20 plus years experience in global drug research and development.

In her 'downtime' Jacqueline likes reading, traveling, spending time with family and friends and listening to music. She is an avid sports fan, especially with anything associated with her beloved NC State Wolfpack and resides in the Raleigh, NC area.

Kim Brown

Kimberley Brown has over 30 years of experience in financial services supporting annuities, mutual funds, flexible spending and other tax deferred programs. Kim has a MBA from Washburn University and maintains her series 6 and 26 licenses. She also holds certifications from the Fellow Life Management Institute, Fellow Life and Health Claims, Associate Customer Service and the Associate, Annuity Products and Administration. Kim has been working with parents and students regarding the college application and scholarship processes for almost 5 years, serving as President of Financial Mastery Experience.

Kim is a member of Delta Sigma Theta, Incorporated and The Links, Incorporated. She is an advocate and voice for children having served on several boards to include past president of the YWCA, Florence Crittenton Home for teenage pregnant mothers as well as many others. She maintains social media pages and groups, "Realizing the College Dream" providing free information regarding the college planning and financing process for a debt free degree.

Kim was the recipient of the Topeka Kansas, Martin Luther King Award in 2008 and YWCA, Woman of the Year nominee in

1999. Most importantly, Kim is a mother to Xavier Dahron Hill. Xavier is a junior at Morehouse College, President of the Junior class and a member of Alpha Phi Alpha, Fraternity, Inc.

Edith Utete

Edith is a devoted wife and mother who loves making a positive impact on other people's lives. She is an author, poet, speaker, trainer, thought leader and lawyer with a keen interest in Broadcasting, Space, Cyber, Telecommunications and Intellectual Property laws. She is a member of the Zimbabwe Academic Research Network (ZARNet) Board and a resident columnist on quintessentialf.com, a platform for empowerment and encouragement of women through the word of God.
Edith is also very passionate about the protection of children and is always exploring ways of safeguarding the interests of children. As the Founder of DigitalAgeConversations, she gives advice on safe, responsible and legal internet use to parents, children, educators and businesses and raises awareness on the effects of technology on children and young people. Edith is also one of the current Chapter Leads for Women in Tech Africa in Zimbabwe and is a mentor for girls in STEM as one of the founding members of Women4STEM.

She seeks to inspire other women and children with her spiritual, personal and professional experiences and is a contributor to the Women in Law Connect initiative which seeks to inform, inspire, empower and elevate female lawyers. She is a contributing author to in a book called Tales of Womanhood that has inspirational and motivational messages for women from across the globe. She is an eternal student who loves the outdoors, travelling, reading and spending time with her family and close friends.

Taren Kinebrew

Taren R. Kinebrew is the founder & CEO of Sweet Petit Desserts, a successful bakery in Cincinnati, OH. She is the mother of a beautiful teen daughter and wife to her high school sweetheart. After leaving Corporate America in 2008, Taren decided to use her business skills and talents as a 3rd generation baker to birth a business to bring Love & Happiness to her clients. Taren's mantra is "You deserve a treat as long as it is sweet and petit," which is what led her to create her delectable treats in small portions. Taren graduated with honors from North Carolina Central University with a B.B.A. in CIS and Minor in Accounting in 1998. She served in the Army National Guard while obtaining her Bachelors degree and working as a programmer/analyst for IBM. Taren has received several awards including: Cincy Chic Woman of the Year Award 2017, PTIO Global Smasher Award 2016, BCWN Entrepreneur Award 2015, Finalist for the Martha Stewart American Made Contest, Featured in Cincinnati Wedding Magazine, Cincinnati Chamber of Commerce WE Business to Watch & Over The Rhine Chamber of Commerce Star Award. She is actively involved in the community and has been 2013 & 2014 Chair of St Vincent de Paul Retrofitting's Annual Event. She has been interviewed for TV segments on Cincinnati's Fox Morning Show, sharing her expertise in business and baking.

Website: www.sweetpetitdesserts.com
Email: taren@sweetpetitdesserts.com

Patra Smith

Patra is the CEO and president of multiple successful commercial and industrial maintenance repair companies, she is also a certified solution-focused life coach, yoga and meditation instructor. As Patra continue's to sustain her thriving companies she pours her self into her purpose by inspiring others to reach life changing breakthroughs though her Motivational Speaking,Writing and her own self conduct. Patra uses her website as a platform to share her God inspired Messages, She uses her messages as a way to uplift people, guiding them to a mindset to "Overcome their trials instead of becoming their trials", She also lives In the truth of "when she blesses others, she blesses herself and as she inspires others she opens the door to be inspired also!" She uses her knowledge and experience of the mind, body and spirit to help people discover God within them selves. Patra combines exercising the mind, daily spiritual alignment habits and mindfulness of what enters the body to help people claim heirship to their own divine Godlike essence. Patra is on a Mission to help people Realize their very own Atman, which in her own definition she describes as "The inner soul that resides in all of us, the greater/higher essence of our selves that is directly connected to God." She believe's through self work, smelting and keeping aligned with God's direct channel of energy we all can reach a point of having the most divine essence of our selves predominant in our daily walk as "God's expressions". Patra speaks of this and more in her upcoming book "Atman Being, Being God Daily". Learn more about Patra and her messages on Patrasmessage.com and follow her on instagram @ patrasmessage.

Nikki Miller

Nikki W. Miller is a passionate Educator where she serves as an Assistant Principal at a High School in Greenville, NC. Nikki attended Spelman College where she completed her Freshman and Sophomore years and The University of North Carolina at Chapel Hill where she earned a Bachelor of Science Degree. She later earned a Master of Science Degree in School Administration and Curriculum Instruction from East Carolina University. She is currently enrolled at Northcentral University where she is a Ed.D. Candidate - Organizational Leadership. Nikki is an active member of Delta Sigma Theta Sorority, Inc. where she serves in the Greenville (NC) Alumnae Chapter through service projects for the community. She is an advocate for the American Heart Association where she has served planning Red Dress Events and a participant in the Down East Heart Walk, raising awareness that heart disease is the #1 killer of women in America. She has been a faithful member and servant at her church Sycamore Hill Missionary Baptist Church in Greenville, NC. She is the wife of Anthony and the very proud mother of two young adult daughters, Gabrielle Nicole Miller, JD who is a Legislative Correspondent for the office of Congresswoman Frederica Wilson (Florida) where she serves in the Unites States

Capitol in Washington, D.C. and Moriah Joelle Miller who is a Junior at North Carolina State University in Raleigh, N.C. where she is a 2020 Bachelor of Science Candidate in Sport Management. Nikki enjoys coming home each day after busy days at work to her 2 year old Shih Tzu dog named Macey Ann Miller. Nikki is an entrepreneur as an Independent Consultant with Paparazzi Jewelry and Accessories. You can find beautiful $5 and $25 Signature Collection bling on her website at www. jewelswithnikki.com. Above all, she is a child of the Most High King, and is in hot pursuit of the purpose, calling, and destiny God Almighty has ordained for her life!

Sherika Jernigan

Sherika is the owner and director of All Kids Matter turtoring seevices. A program providing extra after school help for Pre-k - 3rd grades students. When she isn't lending her services, she enjoys being a mom and a active member at Hines Chapel AME. Sherika is currently in the beginners ministry class Joshua 101. She aspire to encourage women to break the silence.

Rhonda Glover

Rhonda M. Glover was born in Annapolis, Maryland and raised in Washington, DC. She graduated from Old Dominion University in Norfolk, Virginia and received a Bachelor of

Science degree in Criminal Justice. She subsequently received a Master's of Science degree in Management from the Johns Hopkins University in Baltimore, Maryland. Ms. Glover is currently enrolled at the Grand Canyon University in Phoenix, Arizona pursuing a Doctor of Education in Organizational Leadership with an emphasis in Organizational Development. She also holds a certificate in Nonprofit Executive Management from the Georgetown University in Washington, DC.

She began her career with the Federal Bureau of Investigation (FBI) in August 1984 assigned to FBI Headquarters (FBIHQ) in the Technical Services Division. In 1985, she was promoted to the Laboratory Division as a Photographer. In January 1987, Ms. Glover was promoted to the New York Office as an Investigative Specialist assigned to the Special Surveillance Group working Foreign Counterintelligence matters. In September 1988, she was appointed to the position of Special Agent.

Upon completion of training, she was assigned to the Newark Field Division investigating drug violations. While in the Newark Division, Ms. Glover was a member of its inaugural Evidence Response Team and worked major investigations such as TWA 800 and UNABOM. In July 1998, Ms. Glover transferred to the Washington Field Office and continued to investigate drug matters. In March 2000, Ms. Glover was promoted to Supervisory Special Agent assigned to FBIHQ, Criminal Investigative Division, Drug Section, Colombian/Caribbean Unit, She was subsequently assigned to the Inspection Management Unit, Inspection Division. In June 2005, she was promoted to the Newark Division to oversee a traditional Organized Crime matters. In October 2006, she initiated an Intelligence Program squad of Special Agents focusing on the development of Human Intelligence.

In September 2009, Ms. Glover was promoted to Assistant Special Agent in Charge (ASAC) of the New Haven Field Office overseeing the National Security Branch, which was comprised of the Counterintelligence, Counterterrorism, Cyber and Intelligence programs. From October 2011-March 2015, she served as the Criminal/Administrative Branch ASAC with program management responsibilities for Violent Crime, White Collar Crime, Violent Gangs, Public Corruption, Violent Crimes Against Children, Financial Management and Support Services. She also served as the New Haven Division's Leadership Coordinator and Compliance Officer. In March 2015, Ms. Glover was assigned to the Human Resources Division, FBIHQ in Washington, DC where she continues to lead special projects related to human resource matters. She served as the Acting Unit Chief with oversight of the Onboarding New Employees Program, a program to assist new employees in the navigation of their first year of employment with the FBI. Ms. Glover currently serves as the Program Manager for the Professional Development Program in the FBI's Human Resources Division where she is responsible for the delivery of professional development content.

Ms. Glover is a Life member of the National Organization of Black Law Enforcement Executives (NOBLE) where, since 2002, she has served as the NOBLE National Youth Committee Chairperson. She is also a charter member of the Connecticut

Chapter of NOBLE which was initiated in 2010. As the youth committee chairperson, Ms. Glover singlehandedly developed its acclaimed annual youth leadership conference which has impacted more than 2500 youth. She is also a member of the International Association of Chiefs of Police (IACP), where she served on the Human and Civil Rights Committee. In 2008, through the Civil Rights Committee, she developed the IACP's onsite community service and Explorers Project which is executed yearly during its annual conferences. As a result of her work with IACP, she was appointed to the National Law Enforcement Exploring Committee. Ms. Glover is a member of the Police Executive Research Forum, and attended Session 72 of the Law Enforcement Executive Development Seminar where she is a member of its association. Other membership organizations include being a Diamond Life member of Delta Sigma Theta Sorority, Incorporated, a Life member of the National Association of the Advancement of Colored People, and the National Council of Negro Women. Ms. Glover is a member of the Society for Human Resource Management and serves on the Executive Board for the Warford Foundation which was founded to assist military widows and single mothers with the opportunity to further their education in nursing. In September 2012, she was selected to participate in the prestigious Masters Series for Distinguished Leaders through the Skinner Leadership Institute, a program designed to empower leaders in Washington, DC. She is a member of the International Coach Federation and holds certifications from the World Coach Institute as a Career Coach, and a certification from the Youth Coaching Institute as a Youth Mentor Coach with a focus on ages 14-30. In May 2016, she was selected to represent the FBI at Harvard University, John F. Kennedy School of Government participating in "Women and Power: Leadership in the New World," an intense, interactive experience designed to help women advance to top positions of influence in public leadership.

In September 2007, Ms. Glover was presented with the FBI Director's Award for Equal Employment Opportunity in recognition of her leadership, training, recruitment, and significant contributions to enhance employment opportunities for women and minorities within the FBI. The FBI Director's Award is one of the highest forms of recognition received by an FBI employee. Ms. Glover is the recipient of the 2009 Women of Achievement Award presented by the Central Jersey Alumnae Chapter of the Delta Sigma Theta Sorority, Incorporated. She was also recognized by the Western Region, New Jersey of American Society for Industrial Security with the Leadership Award for her service to the community. In May 2017, Ms. Glover received an Honorary Doctorate in Humanitarian Services from the Lincoln College of New England and was its first female commencement day in the 50 year history of the school. She currently resides in Washington, DC.

Carla McNeal

Carla McNeal is a self-proclaimed Southern Belle who has found herself in the middle of the DMV (D.C., Maryland, Virginia) area due to her husband's career in the United States Navy. A native of the great state of Alabama (War Eagle!), she has been an educator since 2004, having been a teacher, department chair, executive director, and she currently serves as an assistant principal. In 2017, Carla defended her dissertation entitled, Empowered Intersectionality Among Black Female School Leaders: A Transcendental Phenomenological Study, which unpacked the multiple nuances of the double-minority status of Black women school leaders. A member of several professional organizations, her passion is working with underperforming teachers to help them become better practitioners in the classroom. She is a worship leader at her church and loves to spend time volunteering at the church with her husband, Cedric. In her spare time, Carla repurposes and reimagines furniture and knick-knacks to be used in other ways; one of her many dreams is to own a home staging company as a side business.

Above all, Carla considers her marriage to be her first ministry and enjoys talking to women about the transforming power of applying biblical truths to marriage and family issues.

To Be Continued…

Dear Fear Teen Edition Coming Fall 2018

Dear Fear Volume 3 Coming Spring 2019

For More Information

Visit www.YourNextIsNow.Com

31447908R00126

Made in the USA
Columbia, SC
08 November 2018